THE PASTOR'S

Funeral Planner

THOMAS H. HERMIZ
STAN TOLER

BEACON HILL PRESS
OF KANSAS CITY

Copyright 2011
by Thomas H. Hermiz, Stan Toler, and
Beacon Hill Press of Kansas City

ISBN 978-0-8341-2723-4

Printed in the United States of America

Cover Design: J.R. Caines
Interior Design: Sharon Page

Library of Congress Cataloging-in-Publication Data

Hermiz, Tom, 1938-
    The pastor's funeral planner / Thomas H. Hermiz and Stan Toler.
        p. cm.
    Includes bibliographical references.
    ISBN 978-0-8341-2723-4 (pbk.)
    1. Funeral service—Planning. 2. Funeral rites and ceremonies—
Planning. 3. Church work with the bereaved. I. Toler, Stan. II. Title.
    BV199.F8H47 2011
    265'.85—dc23
                                                            2011022344

10 9 8 7 6 5 4 3 2 1

In loving memory of Karen Hermiz,
daughter of Tom Hermiz,
and William Aaron Toler, father of Stan Toler.

Contents

Acknowledgments

Special thanks to Nazarene Publishing House and the entire team of Beacon Hill Press of Kansas City. Special thanks also to Jerry Brecheisen.

Introduction

A pastor recently said, "I would rather do funerals than weddings any day."

He explained: "At weddings the only thing anyone remembers are the words 'I do' and 'You may kiss the bride.'"

Some pastors may agree with that; others don't. The fact remains that a funeral service is an opportune—and God-ordained—time for clergy to share a word of hope to those who are numbed by loss and wondering where God is in the midst of their pain. Like David, they cry out, "Has God forgotten to be merciful? Has he in anger withheld his compassion?" (Psalm 77:9).

Pastor, you are God's spokesperson for such a time as this. Whether your audience numbers in the tens or hundreds, what you say from the first moments of the funeral service has the potential of bringing people closer to each other and to God.

When death interrupts life, we are reminded of life's brevity and the looming presence of eternity. From our experience in ministry, we know the excruciating moments when a pastor must guide a family through the most difficult loss on earth. You will too. As you sit and listen and pray and weep with them, you will often feel inadequate to deal with the level of pain they are enduring.

As one who serves in a place of ministry to those who are grieving, you are called upon to be ready on short notice:

- You consult with families with diverse needs and raw emotions.

- You face difficult moments with loved ones, and having resources on hand to aid you in your preparation is crucial to your own sense of calm and purpose.
- You need a user-friendly reference book for funeral service preparation.

During our combined years of ministry we have cared for seemingly countless numbers of people. Yet we know what it is like to search for good materials, for relevant expressions of compassion, and application of God's Word.

What follows is a comprehensive manual of resources to bring meaning and order to a very common ministry moment. The funeral tradition spans history to that heartwarming scene on a mountaintop overlooking the Promised Land when the Creator himself gave the eulogy of one of His most beloved servants. Deuteronomy 34:1-6 records the ceremony:

> Then Moses climbed Mount Nebo from the plains of Moab to the top of Pisgah, across from Jericho. There the LORD showed him the whole land— from Gilead to Dan, all of Naphtali, the territory of Ephraim and Manasseh, all the land of Judah as far as the western sea, the Negev and the whole region from the Valley of Jericho, the City of Palms, as far as Zoar. Then the LORD said to him, "This is the land I promised on oath to Abraham, Isaac and Jacob when I said, 'I will give it to your descendants.' I have let you see it with your eyes, but you will not cross over into it." And Moses the servant of the LORD died there in Moab, as the LORD had said. He buried him in Moab, in the valley opposite Beth Peor, but to this day no one knows where his grave is.

Often in the course of theological training, some of the most common ministry practices are given relatively incidental coverage. A friend of ours told of a telephone call from a recent seminary graduate who said, "I have a funeral this week, and I don't know at which end of the casket I should stand."

Sadly, many pastors have had those embarrassing moments when they had to take a cue from the funeral director in order to calm their own nerves about funeral etiquette. Of course, no seminary can prepare the ministry candidate for every situation in ministry life—and, of course, it is always proper to ask questions of another professional. But just as some professions offer refresher courses, this book can serve as a reminder of the characteristics of a meaningful funeral service.

We also want to offer you a fresh look at some of the traditional facets of the service. Some things cannot be improved on, however. The instruction, encouragement, and compassionate messages of the eternal Word of God are as fresh today as they were in Temple worship times in the Old Testament.

When you are called upon to plan a funeral service, this book will be a good place to start your research. In it you will find—

- Age-related sermons
- Sermons for honoring public servants
- Sermons for crisis situations
- Contemporary and classic committal services
- Contemporary and classic quotations
- Illustrations
- Readings
- Lyrics to beloved hymns
- Scripture readings
- Prayers and benedictions
- Grief care resources

- Tips for counseling the bereaved
- Funeral etiquette
- Tips for outreach and assimilation

As you become the voice and heart of God to those who are walking in the valley of the shadow of death, we pray that you may sense the blessing and presence of the Holy Spirit. We also pray that your words will be filled with the love of Christ and that you will be His representative to those who mourn.

Section One
The Funeral Service

Purpose of the Funeral
Funeral Customs
Funeral Etiquette
Records

1

Purpose of the Funeral

Why should a family plan a funeral service? Some cultures skip the ceremonies and bury their dead immediately without any sermons, special music, or eulogies.

What is the common denominator that unites Christians in formally memorializing the life of another? Bennett and Foley explain, "Funerals and memorial services gather the community around the grieving family and friends. There is nothing more consoling to those nearest to the person who has died than to realize how much their loved one was loved by others. Often it even comes as a surprise to the family to discover just how far afield the person's influence had spread."[1]

The funeral service, then—

- Gives emotional closure.
- Honors the deceased.
- Encourages the survivors.
- Motivates the faith community.
- Highlights human relationships.
- Recognizes shared gifts.

Observing these principles gives the officiating clergy a blueprint for planning the service—in pastoral calling, sermon preparation, Scripture reading, and preparing the eulogy.

Funeral services reflect the basic beliefs of the faith community. For example, Stuart Matlins summarized some of the principles found in a funeral service he attended in a local church:

The Church of the Nazarene affirms that life is eternal, that through faith in Christ one can look forward to life with God after death. Death may be a time of separation from the body, but the soul and new body will be reunited upon the coming of Christ and the final judgment. Funerals have as their purpose: (1) expressing grief and comforting one another in our bereavement, (2) celebrating the life of the deceased, and (3) affirming faith in life with God after death.[2]

Funeral services allow the pastor and congregation to minister to friends and family members of the deceased. The care—and prayer—surrounding the church's participation in a funeral is a time of connection. In one sense, the funeral is a bridge of communication of love and concern and the message of eternal life through faith in the Lord Jesus Christ.

The funeral acknowledges God's creation and care. A funeral service is a defining mark in the line of life that is ordained by God. Thomas G. Long wrote about the spiritual truths that should be reflected in a Christian funeral. He said the place of disposition of the body "is not simply a grave or a cremation furnace. It's a place of farewell where we, with thanksgiving and tears, hand the one God has given us back into the trust of God." He concludes by saying that the Christian funeral is a "proclamation of the gospel: that we are loved by God and that we are travelling toward God."[3]

Your funeral ministry is an opportunity to be an ambassador of God's kingdom, to—

- Determine that the funeral service will bring honor to the Lord Jesus Christ.
- Remind the survivors of both the certainty of death and the hope of eternal life.

- Ask the Holy Spirit to give you words that will express God's kindness in difficult situations.
- Be sensitive to opportunities for sharing the promises of God's Word.

2

Funeral Customs

Honoring the dead is manifested in every generation and culture. From the earliest civilizations the need to grieve has been recognized. The ancient Egyptians adorned the walls of buildings and tombs with their colorful hieroglyphs, often portraying the significant events in a person's life and the manner of his or her death. Their fascination with the passage from death to eternity is demonstrated in the great number of mummies they left behind.

While not every people group practiced mummifying, every society has had rituals for dealing with death and grief. Some of these seem primitive and unrefined to us today, but maybe it's because we would rather ignore death than process it.

Traditions of Mourning

The Gaelic peoples, most notably the Irish and the Scottish, practiced the tradition of *keening* or *wailing* at the bedside of the deceased. This form of vocal lament may have contained poetic descriptions of the departed loved one or expressions of mourning for those left behind. It was often accompanied by rocking or kneeling or clapping. Sometimes a woman or chorus of women were paid to provide this expected form of mourning. In fact, the commonly heard phrase "wail like a Banshee" refers to the mythical Irish spirit of death who was believed to be an omen of death and emitted a unique, mournful cry. Some countries in the Middle East and Africa still employ the use of public mourners to chant and rock over the bodies of the dead.

In the England of Charles Dickens' day, the use of mutes was common. A mute was a person hired to be a symbolic protector of the deceased; he or she wore a black coat, hat, and gloves and stood near the door of the home or church with a sad, mournful face.

In many cultures dark colors have long been associated with mourning. Though wearing black as a symbolic expression of grief dates back to the Roman Empire, it was in nineteenth-century England that mourning behavior developed into a complex pattern of rules. The heavy garments a woman in mourning was expected to wear became known as "widow's weeds." The Old English word *waed* means *garment*. There was even special jewelry for mourning, such as a locket containing a lock of the deceased person's hair. There were also restrictions on social activities for those in mourning.

Queen Victoria's reign saw the culmination of formal mourning. During this time, proper dress and conduct for the grieving period became very important. In America the antebellum South also embraced many traditions of mourning, as they adhered to a strict code of conduct in every circumstance.

Many symbols of mourning were in use during this era. Black armbands were worn by men in military service or the servants of one who had died. Funerary wreaths and black crepe paper on the front door informed the community that death had visited a family.

Hair art was practiced by women in the eighteenth and nineteenth centuries as a work of love and tribute to the deceased. The hair of a loved one was woven into wreaths, palette work, table work, and hair art pictures. The designs were elaborate, and it took hours to create these special projects.

While some of these ideas may seem distasteful and silly to the modern mind, they allowed the family to observe an expected routine of grief that society not only understood but also encouraged. Grief was part of the landscape of life, and people allowed room for its presence and expression.

Twenty-first-century funerals may follow none of the customs just mentioned. As an advanced culture, we may not be as comfortable with extended expressions of grief. Indeed, we may not have the time or temperament for it. Our lives are too busy and too forward-thinking to allow the indulgence of mourning. However, that has not helped us.

Packaging Grief

As a society, we don't mind flying the flag at half-staff or observing a moment of silence at public events, but prolonged outpourings of mourning tend to make us feel uncomfortable. We have become good at packaging grief in a three- or four-day event that concludes with a church dinner and a flurry of cards and flowers.

Though we have psychiatrists and therapists to help us understand emotions, we are very uncomfortable sitting next to someone who is crying. We feel we have to say something, fix something, or do something. Pastors are especially susceptible to this syndrome, for they are the "fixers" of the Church world; they feel driven to offer solutions. Yet many times grief doesn't require words—it requires permission and presence.

Permission to Grieve

As a culture, we must give ourselves and our friends and loved ones permission to grieve a loss. Just as we would allow a friend to be happy when something wonderful happens, we must make peace with tears that are shed when something terrible occurs. Grief is a natural and necessary experience, and avoiding or concealing it does not erase its effect. When we learn to accept the presence of grief, we will be healthier in our emotional approach to life.

There is nothing wrong with weeping at the loss of someone we loved. We may need to redefine our expectations of appropriate grieving to be more in line with Jesus' sorrow over the loss of His friend, Lazarus, and His actions of consolation that followed (John 11).

- Jesus wept with the loved ones and went to them.
- Jesus expressed His concern in words of comfort.
- Jesus expressed hope in the face of death.
- Jesus spoke of life beyond the grave.
- Jesus gave glory to His Heavenly Father.

As an officiating member of the clergy, you will find that the Jesus model will serve you best, and it will help you as you serve others. The funeral service is another opportunity for you to be Christlike.

3

Funeral Etiquette

While funeral customs and ceremonies may change with the times, the presence of the clergy should reflect the unchanging dignity and compassion of the profession. What follows are some guidelines to follow when you're asked to conduct a funeral.

Attitude/Decorum

Relaxed professionalism should be the order of the day, and the event calls for your best and kindest behavior.

Dress

In almost every case, business dress is best. Neatness reflects your ministry and the ministry of the church or organization you represent.

Responsibilities

You are the manager of the funeral service in cooperation with the funeral director and participants. Your gentle guidance in carrying out the order of service will enhance the ceremony and result in pleasant memories for the survivors.

Order of Service

The order of service should be planned (and written out) in advance of the service and should honor special requests of family members if at all possible. Copies of the service order that you have checked for spelling and sequence should be given to the funeral director, musicians, and other service participants.

Inspection Details

After arriving at the funeral chapel or church auditorium, officiating clergy should be responsible for inspecting the arrangement of clergy seating, sound system equipment, and the participation of other clergy or guests. It is also advisable to look for the nearest restroom and a quiet place where you can prepare yourself in advance of the service.

Family Gathering/Prayer

It is customary for clergy to meet with the family prior to the service. Check with the funeral director in advance to see what arrangements have been made for the pre-service meeting. The pre-service prayer gives you an opportunity to express your concern, and your compassionate spirit gives you an opportunity to make a first impression that may result in further ministry.

Processional

Out of courtesy to the family and respect for the deceased, stand when the casket is moved to the front of the chapel or auditorium and/or as family members are ushered to their reserved seating. In cases when the casket is moved to the front of the auditorium, you should lead the processional.

Placement

The service should be conducted from behind the supplied lectern with attention given to voice clarity and projection. Periodic glimpses at the service order will help you in cueing other participants of the service who have been advised of your cues in advance.

Service Flow

Most funeral services average twenty to thirty minutes in length, except for graveside services, which are often shorter. Services that are too lengthy or too short are uncomfortable for those attending. Lengthy sermons or homilies should be avoided. To keep the service flowing, participants should be advised to follow other participants in the service without introduction by giving attention to their printed order of service and/or cues from officiating clergy.

Conclusion

The funeral service ends with the benediction and in most cases signals the funeral director either to close the casket or to usher guests from the chapel or auditorium. You will then take your place at the head of the casket until it is transported to the hearse for the committal service. In cases of inclement weather, you may do the committal service before the body is transported. In some cases, you will give the announcements and directives about the family dinner that is to follow the committal service.

If the body has been cremated, the benediction and possible announcement of a family dinner will immediately follow the benediction.

Recessional

You will lead the casket and pallbearers to the hearse and stand by until the pallbearers have loaded the casket into the hearse.

Graveside Service

Once the funeral procession has reached the graveside, you will proceed to the hearse and stand and wait as pallbearers remove the casket. Then you will lead the casket and pallbearers to the gravesite, standing at the head of the casket or as advised by the funeral director. Once the casket is in place and family members are seated, the funeral director will cue you to begin the service, which should be brief, with Scripture reading, poem or reading, and committal.

Greeting Family Members

Following the committal, you should go to the seated family members and greet each one with a handshake and/ or brief expression of concern. It is also advisable for you to remain at the graveside until the family has said their last good-byes.

Family Dinners/Church Ministry

If a family dinner has been arranged, plan to attend if possible. Family dinners are a good time to connect with those who participated in the funeral. Attention should be given to make sure the dinner is running smoothly and that the needs of the guests are being met. Attention should also be given to communicating continual care and availability to family members.

Professionalism and courtesy, mixed with friendliness and compassion, are characteristics that will endear you to family and friends of the deceased.

Military Funeral Graveside Service

- The hearse arrives at the gravesite. The soldiers present arms.
- The casket team secures the casket.
- The chaplain will lead the way to the casket, followed by the casket team.
- The casket team sets down the casket and secures the flag.
- The flag is stretched out and centered over the casket.
- The chaplain, military or civilian, performs the interment service.
- A gun salute is fired (for those eligible) before the benediction.
- The chaplain concludes the service and backs away.
- A rifle volley is initiated and completed.
- The bugler plays "Taps."
- The casket team folds the flag and presents it to the commanding officer
- The casket team leaves the gravesite.
- The flag is presented to the next-of-kin.[1]

4

Records

As the officiating clergy, you are responsible for maintaining records of funeral services as well as participating in official signatures.

Clergy Card

In most cases, the funeral director will supply clergy with a record of the funeral that gives the legal name of the deceased and the date of the funeral service. This record should be kept for future reporting or reference and for information purposes in ongoing care.

Funeral Service Records

Individual funeral service records may also be kept for reporting to your denomination, for future follow-up, for tracking sermons, or for follow-up correspondence records such as the anniversary of the death. Many church membership software programs contain modules for recording weddings and funerals, or you may want to create your own spreadsheet in which to file your records. Your database should contain the following information:

- Name of the deceased
- Date of death
- Immediate family survivors
- Spouse, father, mother, children, siblings, other connections or contacts
- Correspondence (type, date)

- Date of the funeral or memorial service
- Location of the funeral and gravesite
- Sermon title, scripture
- Scripture reading
- Music

Information Checklist

You may want to assist family members of the deceased in compiling information for the funeral service. The following list is suggested. It may not be complete, and it does not substitute for legal information demanded by your state.

Funeral Arrangements
- Preferred funeral home
- Preferred funeral director
- Favorite songs
- Favorite scripture
- Cemetery services
- Disposition of remains (burial or cremation)

Personal Information of the Deceased
- Full name and nickname
- Date and place of birth
- Parents' names
- Spouse's name, date of birth
- Children's names, dates of birth
- Previous marriages
- Education
- Honors
- Notable achievements

Church Affiliation
- Name of church
- Pastor's name

- Member or attendee
- Date of membership
- Titles
- Service or responsibilities

Other

- Organization memberships
- Social Security number
- Estate plan or will
- Executor information
- Living will
- Power of attorney
- Attorney
- Cemetery plot deed
- Safe deposit box, location, number, key
- Post office box, location, key
- Automobile titles
- Birth certificates
- Passport
- Tax records
- Life insurance policies (personal or work-related)
- Checking account
- Mortgage papers/deeds storage location
- Newspaper or publication information
- Funeral home information
- Burial clothing preference
- Open or closed casket preference
- Gravestone preference
- Flowers preference
- Music preference
- Officiating clergy preference
- Notification—friends, family, associates
- Death certificate distribution list

- Hobbies/special interests[1]

Good records prompt you to good follow-up. The recording of names and other information will be valuable to you in your ongoing care and efforts to assimilate friends and family into your local ministry.

Section Two
Planning the Funeral Service

Orders of Service
Scripture Readings
Eulogies
Sermons and Sermon Outlines
Poems and Other Readings
Illustrations
Committals

5

Orders of Service

The funeral service can be a meaningful time for family members and friends. An orderly and efficiently planned and conducted service can have a lasting impact. Remember: it is more than a ritual—it is memorializing the life of someone whose loss has brought grief to another.

Personalizing the Funeral

A hundred years ago, funerals were pretty standard in nature. There were solemn words, somber music, black clothing, thrown flowers, and the familiar "ashes to ashes."

Not anymore. And that is good in many ways.

While there is inherent dignity in the age-old rituals, personal touches give the family the opportunity to publicly honor their loved one and more properly represent the life now gone.

Photos
- The use of photo memory boards, scrapbooks, and video tributes is common. By displaying images of significant moments in their loved one's life, families can share their special pride in what made him or her so special.
- Viewing portraits of the deceased in younger days helps those attending understand who the person was and fosters a deeper connection with their life. An older person is seen in a different light when one

observes the youthful beauty or vigor of their earlier years; it reminds us that aging is a journey that all of us must take.

- Digital video tributes are fairly easy to create and can be set to music and viewed on a small screen in the waiting area or shown during the service itself.

- Some families may choose to have a favorite photo made into a painted portrait.

Music

- Most people associate music with funerals, and an obvious way to personalize the service is to have favorite songs played or sung. With the wide scope of music styles today, there are likely to be a few unusual selections chosen for a funeral from time to time. Sometimes the songs don't seem to suit a funeral setting, but as with weddings, those planning the service have the final say.

Flowers/Contributions

- Flowers have long been an accepted way to honor the deceased and express love to the family. Some families are opting to have contributions made in their loved one's name to a favorite charity or organization. While this is certainly a legitimate request and entirely within the family's discretion, it is important to understand that a funeral with no flowers may look very forlorn and unimportant. Families may later regret the fact that there were few or no floral arrangements at such a special time. In fact, recent research suggests that flowers improve emotional health, feed compassion, and fight anxiety. It is also healthy for friends to be able to express their support through the tangible gift of flowers.[1] An artful florist can even create personalized arrangements that reflect the interests of the deceased or coordinate the color of the floral casket spray with the frame of a special photo. If you as the pastor are asked for advice on this matter, it might be prudent to suggest they offer the alternative of donations but that they not exempt friends from sending flowers as well. Care can be taking in wording the statement so that it gives a clear message of the family's wishes.

Keepsakes

- In addition to the traditional obituary cards with scripture that have long been in use, families today may also choose to give out bookmarks or memorial folders personalized with a photo of the loved one. Sometimes the design or theme of these materials is based on a personal hobby or interest of the deceased. The family may also choose to give out "favors," pieces of a favorite candy, or cards bearing a favorite recipe of the deceased.

Sharing Memories

Families draw comfort from memories of the departed loved one, and it is a joy to hear others recount their special memories as well. People use memories in several ways to personalize the funeral service.

- Within the traditional guestbook, families may want to provide a space for those attending to jot down a special memory next to their names.
- Many funeral homes provide an online guest register where people may leave personal notes and comments.
- Some families may request those gathered to write down a favorite memory on slips of paper to be read

during the service or gathered for keeping by the family.

- Still others may have a designated time slot during the service for those in attendance to come forward or stand and verbally share their memories or pay a personal tribute.

Each of these methods makes a contribution to a more personal way to honor the one who has died.

Additional Ways to Personalize the Service

Some families now choose casket cap panels to express the individualism of the deceased. A special emblem or scene may be added to the panel of the casket to further personalize the memory of the loved one.

Orders of Service Samples

Traditional
- Prelude music
- Reading of obituary
- Special vocal music
- Prayer
- Scripture
- Sermon/Eulogy by pastor
- Special song or hymn
- Prayer
- Postlude music

Contemporary
- Prelude music (recorded or live—favorites)
- Special musical selection
- Media presentation (video, PowerPoint, audio)
- Poem or reading
- Scripture reading
- Eulogy/Homily from pastor

- Sharing time (open to friends and family who desire)
- Prayer
- Postlude music

Memorial Service

When a memorial service is conducted following the burial or cremation of the diseased, a portrait, overhead slide, or video may be displayed in a chapel or auditorium where family and friends gather. The order of service may include the following.

- Prelude
- Processional
- Clergy
- Honorary pallbearers
- Family members
- Introduction: Scripture reading and prayer
- Congregational song
- Media presentation
- Eulogies by family and friends
- Musical selection
- Sermon
- Congregational song
- Honors presentation (military)
- Benediction
- Postlude

Memorial Service for the Pre-born

A service for a miscarried or stillborn child need not be long, but it should be meaningful. After all, the child has not lived long enough to have accomplishments or to impact the world at large, but his or her intrinsic worth is something to honor, and the value of that life to God and the parents is inestimable.

If the parents wish to name the child, it will facilitate the needed grieving process and help them feel that this little life was affirmed.

A memorial service of this nature might consist of a simple graveside service or a private ceremony at a funeral home. It could include—

- Prelude
- Introduction: Scripture reading
- Prayer
- Music selection
- Eulogies from clergy, family, or friends
- Selected Scripture readings and comforting words by clergy
- Benediction

6

Scripture Readings

Old Testament Readings

- Genesis 49:29-33
- 1 Kings 2:1-3, 10
- Job 1:21
- Job 5:26
- Job 9:25-26
- Job 19:21-27
- Psalm 16
- Psalm 23
- Psalm 27
- Psalm 39
- Psalm 42
- Psalm 46
- Psalm 71:17-20
- Psalm 90
- Psalm 116
- Psalm 121
- Psalm 130
- Psalm 139:1-17
- Ecclesiastes 3:1-8
- Ecclesiastes 8:8
- Ecclesiastes 12:1-7
- Isaiah 6:1-3
- Isaiah 25:6-9
- Isaiah 26:6-9
- Isaiah 61:1-3
- Jeremiah 31:15

- Lamentations 3:22-26, 31-33
- Daniel 12:1-3

New Testament Readings

- Matthew 11:25-30
- Mark 10:14-16
- John 5:24-29
- John 6:3-5
- John 6:37-40
- John 11:21-27
- John 14:1-6
- John 17:24
- Acts 10:34-43
- Romans 8:14-19, 34-39
- Romans 14:7-12
- 1 Corinthians 15:20-26, 35-38, 42-44, 51-58
- 2 Corinthians 4:16:5-9
- 2 Corinthians 5:1-10
- Philippians 1:19-26
- 1 Thessalonians 4:13-18
- Hebrews 9:23-28
- James 4:13-15
- 1 Peter 1:24
- 1 John 3:1-2
- 1 John 3:14-16
- Revelation 7:9-17
- Revelation 14:13
- Revelation 20:6
- Revelation 20:11-21:1
- Revelation 21:2-7

7

Eulogies

The word *eulogy* comes from the Greek word *eulogia*, which means "praise." The dictionary defines it as a "commendatory oration or writing especially in honor of one deceased."[1] Delivered by a family member, friend, associate, or the officiating clergy, it can also personalize the funeral service in a very real way.

Sample Eulogies

There are different types of eulogies. Some are based on chronological events in a person's life, while others may be built around shared memories or main points of a special theme. A eulogy may also be a tribute to the accomplishments of the deceased or focus on the legacy he or she is leaving behind.

However it is structured, the purpose of a eulogy is to honor the deceased. Instead of using only a traditional funeral "sermon," some pastors see the value of incorporating special tributes and memories into their speaking time. This may be especially good if the deceased did not leave a clear testimony to his or her spiritual condition or if it is known the person was unsaved. Rather than dwell totally on being prepared for eternity, the minister can at least give the family a little comfort and honor a human life by recounting the favorable attributes of the one who is gone.

In order to prepare and deliver a meaningful eulogy, the one speaking must have some background on the person's life. A pastor should schedule a time to meet with the family the day before the funeral service in order to gather this material. He or she can ask some gentle leading questions to help the family remember the things they loved about the deceased and the memories that stand out in their minds. From that, the pastor can craft a fitting eulogy.

If the pastor is the one giving a blended eulogy and homily, it will probably be in the third person. If it is being given by a family member or friend, it may be more personal. While it is always difficult to be vulnerable in such a sorrowful setting, the trend today is toward a more personal approach to the service.

Sample Eulogy for a Young Adult (Chronological)

Tiffany was a gifted and loving person. As a child, she was active and full of life. From her earliest years, she had an unusual way with animals, loving every stray cat or dog in the community. Her mother lovingly recalls the time Tiffany brought home five stray cats in one day and declared that all of them were going to sleep in her bed.

At the age of ten, Tiffany gave her life to Christ one morning in Sunday School. Mrs. Jones, her teacher, had just given the lesson on the story of Jesus calling the fishermen, James and John, to follow Him. As the little children bowed their heads to pray, Mrs. Jones asked who would like to follow Jesus the rest of their lives, and Tiffany was one who raised her hand. She repeated the prayer with Mrs. Jones and was quick to tell her parents about it after church. Throughout the rest of her life, she continued to follow Jesus and make an impact on those around her.

As a teenager, Tiffany possessed a sparkling personality and quick wit. She became involved in the debate team at her high school, where in the heat of battle she often stumped her opponents with her disarming smile. She was gifted with the ability to speak clearly and intelligently. Tiffany also played the guitar, adding to the music when the church youth group gathered for a bonfire or hayride.

After graduating from high school, Tiffany entered a Christian college, where she pursued a missions degree. Her professors remember her as a respectful, intelligent girl who had a tendency to run a little late but could smile her way out of reprimands. Her fellow students recall her readiness to help others and her zest for life. Everyone she knew was aware that she belonged to Christ; it was a fact of her life.

As Tiffany's family and friends, we are greatly saddened that she was taken from us so soon. But in our sorrow is a Heavenly Father who knows the depth of our pain. He does not tell us we should not hurt, nor does He scold us for missing her. God the Father understands the pain of separation from a child; He was separated from His only Son. Jesus, our Savior, can share our heartache because He once stood and wept at the grave of His good friend Lazarus. The Holy Spirit is called the Comforter, and His presence will be there to strengthen us as we adjust to life without Tiffany.

We know that Tiffany is with Jesus. Second Corinthians 5:8 tells us that to be absent from this body is to be present with the Lord. At this moment, though, we miss her terribly. Tiffany is safe and happy with her Lord. Because sin has marred our earth, death is a fact we cannot escape. Yes, it is unfair, it is tragic, and it breaks our hearts. But in God's Word we read that Jesus' death on the Cross broke the power of death for anyone who puts his or her faith in Him. The apostle Paul declared emphatically in 1 Corinthians 15:54 that death has been "swallowed up" in victory. Christ's resurrection guarantees the resurrection of every believer. He is the "first fruits"—the leader—of those who sleep. Because He lives, Tiffany lives with Him now and for eternity.

Those who put their trust in Christ for salvation will also live. It is hard to see eternity on this earth. We get involved with going to school and paying the mortgage and enjoying everyday life, as we should. That is normal. But when sorrow touches our lives, we remember that, after all, life is only a passing scene, and eternity is what we were made for.

Knowing Tiffany helped each of us see how a life can be surrendered to Christ and reminds us even today that to know Him is to be really prepared for whatever life brings and for eternity.

For those of us who loved Tiffany so much, there will be sad days ahead. We know she is with Jesus, but we miss her presence here with us. We want to see her smile and hear her sparkling voice. We will miss her at our gatherings and long for her companionship in the days to come. What can we do with this seemingly unbearable sorrow?

We can bring it to Jesus. He is a Friend in the dark times and gives strength to those who have none. He understands that we are human and cannot fathom eternity. He took our skin and became human too; He knows about our pain. This is why He came—to fight death for us. He was our champion, our defender. But He is also our Rock and Tower of Support. He does not tell us not to grieve—but rather not to grieve without hope. It is only natural to grieve, but we must not despair. As we shed our tears and embrace this unwanted pain, we will walk with the knowledge that He is with us, and we can pour out our grief to Him time and again.

Tiffany had a favorite hymn. Her parents shared with me that she would often strum this on her guitar and sing softly while she sat on the porch swing. I want to read the words to you.

> *What a Friend we have in Jesus,*
>   *All our sins and griefs to bear!*
> *What a privilege to carry*
>   *Everything to God in prayer!*
> *O what peace we often forfeit,*
>   *O what needless pain we bear,*
> *All because we do not carry*
>   *Everything to God in prayer!*
>   —Joseph M. Scriven

Sample Eulogy for an Older Person (Main Points)

John Smith blessed everyone he met. As a human being and as a family man and friend, he was a joy to know. As we've gathered here to remember him and honor the life he lived, I want to share a few ways that he enriched all of us just by knowing him.

Generosity. John was the soul of generosity. Even as a child, he was eager to share what he had with others. His sisters remember that he shared his lunch with others less fortunate at school. His wife recalls that he gladly gave away his last dime to a person who really needed it.

John was generous with his time too. He always had time to help a neighbor, counsel a grandchild, and volunteer for special projects at church. He once said that he would rather spend hours working for the Lord than days lounging for the devil. He invested his time into his family in big ways, and today his sons and daughters reap the benefits as they have become faithful, godly parents to their own children.

John was generous with praise. He had a good word for everyone and always tried to put the best light on anything that happened. As his pastor, I could always count on a hearty "Good sermon, Pastor" from John, whether it was a masterpiece or not. John's many friends liked to be around him, because his positive spirit made any day seem brighter.

Dependability. One could always count on John. If he said he would do it, it would be done. He was as dependable as the sunrise.

A friend shared a memory about the time John promised to help him with some repair work on his roof. On the day they had set to work, John's old pickup would not start, and his wife had gone into town to do some shopping. This was before the days of cell phones, and there was nothing to do but set out walking. John walked into his friend's driveway just 30 minutes after he was supposed to be there, winded from his walk but ready to work. This is just an example of how he kept his word at any cost.

As a father and grandfather, John did his best to keep his word. He attended his son's Little League games and his daughters' piano recitals. He came to his grandson's Cub Scouts graduation and took his granddaughters to the park for play time. If he promised, he did it.

John was a husband who kept his word to his dear wife. Married for fifty-four years, John and Betty were very much in love. John told Betty every night before he went to sleep, "I love you," and he proved it with his life. He was a faithful and devoted husband.

Simplicity. John was an uncomplicated man who valued the good and simple things in life. He possessed a simple trust in God; he just believed what God said was true and based his life on it.

John had a simple approach to living: love others, and treat them with respect. While he certainly had his own opinions on politics and church affairs and events in the community, he was able to look above the differences and keep the law of love supreme in his manner.

John had a simple faith in the future; he believed in heaven. A few weeks before his death, John told his wife to have a Scripture verse inscribed on his headstone. This is what it says: "For I know whom I have believed, and am persuaded that he is able to keep that which I have committed unto him against that day" (2 Timothy 1:12, KJV).

For John Smith, his life of generosity, dependability, and simplicity has been replaced with the glorious light of eternity. He blessed each of us, and we are now eager to be reunited with him someday in another place, where our companionship will never end.

John's favorite hymn was "Amazing Grace." The words are printed in the folder for you. Please join me in singing it at this time.

8

Sermons and Sermon Outlines

Outlines for a General Service

Dwelling in the House of the Lord

Scripture: Psalm 23

Introduction: This psalm is probably read more than any other in times of grief and difficulty. It is a psalm that gives us hope and comfort.

    I. **The Good Shepherd gives us rest (verse 2).**

    II. **The Good Shepherd revives us (verse 2).**

  III. **The Good Shepherd restores us (verse 3).**

  IV. **The Good Shepherd guides us (verses 3-4).**

    V. **The Good Shepherd comforts us (verse 4).**

  VI. **The Good Shepherd feeds us (verse 5).**

 VII. **The Good Shepherd heals us (verse 5).**

VIII. **The Good Shepherd takes us to His house (verse 6).**

Conclusion: He is preparing a place for us. When He calls us home, we will have nothing to fear.

Christ, Our Source of Strength

Scripture: Philippians 4:13

Introduction: In times of great sorrow and heartache we wonder, *Will we find the strength to keep on going?* Paul gives us the answer in this verse: "I can do all things through Christ who strengthens me" (NKJV).

I. Christ is our source of strength.

A. In ourselves we are weak, but He is strong.

B. When we are in Christ and He is in us, we have divine strength to overcome.

II. Christ strengthens us in two primary ways.

A. Through His Word.

B. Through His Spirit.

Conclusion: Your faith in the resurrection power of Christ will sustain you through every moment of every day. "They that wait upon the LORD shall renew their strength" (Isaiah 40:31, KJV).

The Great Persuasion

Scripture: Romans 8:38-39

Introduction: "For I am persuaded that neither death nor life . . . shall be able to separate us from the love of God which is in Christ Jesus our Lord" (verses 38-39, NKJV).

I. Death cannot separate us from the love of God.

A. For the believer "to die is gain" (Philippians 1:21). We are absent from the body, present with the Lord.

B. Death ushers us into the presence of God.

II. Life cannot separate us from the love of God.

A. Principalities and powers will try to defeat us.

B. Christ in us can defeat all of them.

Conclusion: Nothing can separate us from the love of God when we are in Christ.

Words of Comfort

Scripture: John 14:1-3, 16

Introduction: In this passage Jesus had just shared with His disciples that He must die and return to the Father. They were devastated by this frightening news. Christ was their leader, teacher, and defender. Without Him, they felt extremely vulnerable.

Jesus, understanding their fears, gave them these reassuring words of comfort.

I. **Let not your heart be troubled—because you believe in God.**

From the pages of the Old Testament we understand that God is holy and just. Christ brought to us the new and comforting concept that God is our *Father.* God has no desire to be the "man upstairs." He desires an intimate relationship with us. He wants to be our Father.

When I was a child, at times my father was involved in ministry until late at night. When he wasn't home I found it difficult to sleep. However, the moment I heard his car in the driveway, I fell asleep. His presence brought a sense of security and comfort.

Today some of you are wondering how you will make it without your trusted loved one. Be assured that you will be all right, because you believe in God. You will find His grace to be sufficient. He is your Father. He will not fail you now. You are not alone.

II. **Let not your heart be troubled—because you believe in Christ.**

When you believe in Christ, your level of comfort increases. At the Cross, Christ shed His blood and laid down His life to redeem us. His sacrifice satisfied the justice of

God. If we repent of our sins, God for Jesus' sake forgives us. Through Christ we can have peace with God.

When Christ rose from the grave, He gave us the assurance of life beyond the grave. The grave is not the end. Therefore, we do not grieve as do those who have no hope.

Christianity differs from all other religions in that the Author and Finisher of our faith conquered death. Because He lives, we also shall live.

We also find comfort in the fact that Christ, our high priest, is interceding for us at the right hand of the Father. He is praying that your faith will not fail.

III. Let not your heart be troubled—because in my Father's house are many mansions.

Heaven is a real place that Christ is preparing for all who believe in Him. It is a place in the presence of God our Father. It is a place where there is no night, no sorrow, no pain, and no death. It is a place of peace, safety, and boundless joy.

If we repent and believe on the Lord Jesus Christ, we can spend eternity in this marvelous place called heaven.

IV. Let not your heart be troubled—because Christ has sent us another Comforter.

Jesus said, "I must leave you and return to my Father. However, I will give you another Comforter who will abide within you." This Comforter is the blessed Holy Spirit.

There is a great difference between the earthly ministry of Christ and this, the age of the Holy Spirit. Today we can enjoy the constant, continual indwelling presence of the Holy Spirit.

When we are sick and suffering, He is with us. He is with us when we are grieving and brokenhearted. When we walk through the valley of the shadow of death, we fear no evil, for He will be with us then. When no one else understands, He does.

He is our constant Comforter. By the grace of God, even though it is dark and difficult today, your faith will enable you to be victorious. His grace is sufficient. He is the God of all comfort.

Death Is a Friend

Scripture: Romans 8:18

Introduction: We often regard death as a cold, over-whelming force that takes someone from us at an untimely moment. However, there are occasions when it is a merciful event. When a person has suffered a long time from a debilitating illness, death comes as a friend.

I. **Death is a friend—because it is a release from suffering.**

II. **Death is a friend—because it is a release from all human limitations.**

III. **Death is a friend—because it releases us to receive a great reward.**

Conclusion: Death is our friend because it is not the end but the beginning of eternal life in the presence of God. It is the believer's promotion to glory.

Closing Strong

Scripture: 2 Timothy 4:6-8

Introduction: Paul was nearly seventy years old when he wrote this letter to young Timothy. Paul realized it was now his time to move off the stage of action. He was determined to close strong.

I. **His departure was at hand.**

II. **He had fought a good fight.**

III. He had kept the faith.

IV. He had finished the race.

V. He was anticipating his reward.

Conclusion: Let us determine that we will not limp across the finish line. Let's keep the faith and finish strong.

A Lesson from the Cross

Scripture: Luke 23:43

Introduction: When Jesus responded to the dying thief's confession, He taught some powerful things about life after death. He said, "Today you will be with me in paradise" (verse 43).

I. Death is not the end of our existence.

II. Death releases us instantly into eternity—there is no intermediate state.

III. Death for the believer ushers him or her into the presence of God.

IV. Death for the unbeliever banishes him or her forever from the presence of God.

Conclusion: Hebrews 9:27—"Man is destined to die once, and after that to face judgment."

Comforting Words

Scripture: 1 Thessalonians 4:13-18

Introduction: There is real value in meeting here today to comfort one another with the Word of God.

I. We are comforted with the assurance that Christ will return.

II. We are comforted with the assurance that Christ will return with His saints.

III. **We are comforted with the assurance that we will be caught up together with the Lord and His saints.**

Conclusion: We do not sorrow as those who have no hope. We know that when Christ returns we will be reunited with those who died in the faith.

Suffering Is Just for a While

Scripture: 1 Peter 5:10

Introduction: Writing to believers who were experiencing fiery trials, Peter encouraged them with these words: "And the God of all grace, who called you to his eternal glory in Christ, after you have suffered a little while, will himself restore you and make you strong, firm and steadfast."

I. **Suffering will restore you.**

II. **Suffering will make you strong.**

III. **Suffering will make you firm and steadfast.**

Conclusion: Sooner or later we will all experience the pain that comes with grief. If we will keep our trust in God, He will bring these positive blessings out of our sorrow.

God Is Our Strength

Scripture: Psalm 46

Introduction: Where do we turn to find strength in times of trouble and sorrow? The best place to turn is to the Word of God. It has been tested for centuries and has never failed. Psalm 46 is one of our greatest sources of comfort and hope.

I. **God is our source of strength (verse 1).**

II. **God is always available (verse 1).**

III. **God is in control (verse 10).**

Conclusion: You may feel helpless and have some fear as you face the future. There is no need to panic. God is with you, and He is in control. You will find in Him a sufficiency of strength and grace.

It's Just a Step

Scripture: 1 Samuel 20:1-4

Introduction: This passage reveals a beautiful friendship between David and Jonathan. David was trying to avoid Jonathan's father, Saul, who wanted to kill him. David said, "There is only a step between me and death" (verse 3).

I. **Life is fragile.**

II. **Death is just a step away.**

III. **Death is not the end.**

IV. **Death is our entrance into eternal life.**

Conclusion: Do not let your hearts be troubled" (John 14:3). Christ has conquered death. We have the promise of eternal life.

What Is Your Life?

Scripture: James 4:14

Introduction: When we are young and healthy, we rarely think about the brevity and uncertainty of life. We feel that we are indestructible and will live forever. We make plans for the future with the expectation that our plans will come to pass.

Then come moments like these when a loved one or a family member passes from this life to the next. Suddenly, we are forced to think about the most basic questions of life: *Where did we come from? Why are we here? Where are we going?*

I. Where did we come from? Some would have us believe that we reached our present state through a process of evolution. When I see the chaos and moral confusion this teaching has produced, I am convinced they are wrong. Evolution is only a theory that cannot be proven. In fact, when one looks around, it's difficult to find anything that is evolving forward. On the contrary, everything seems to be wearing out, running down, and dying.

I still believe that "in the beginning God created the heavens and the earth" (Genesis 1:1). He then shaped man in His own image out of the dust of the earth and breathed life into him. This is what gives life meaning and significance.

When we understand that life is a gift from God, it leads us to the question *What was God's purpose in creating us?*

II. Why are we here? Why did God create Adam and Eve? He created them for the purpose of having fellowship with them. So the answer to the question is—we are here to enjoy intimate fellowship with God and to glorify Him by serving His Son. God created us for himself.

Tragically, many live and die having never discovered the reason for their existence. The result is they think they can find fulfillment in wealth, fame, power, and popularity. They could have all these things, but without a relationship with God, they will never find true fulfillment and peace.

Life is short and uncertain. God has given us free will and the ability to make our own decisions. It is His desire that we choose to love and serve Him. The choice is yours. To live life to its fullest we must allow God to be the center of our affections.

III. Where are we going? Where is the life you are now living taking you? The choices and decisions you are making daily are either drawing you closer to God or taking you farther away. You are the only one who can decide which road you will travel. There are only two choices.

If you are not at peace with the direction of your life, this would be a good day to covenant with God that you will earnestly seek to know Him on an intimate basis. If you need to change the direction of your life, God will give you the strength and grace to make the necessary adjustments. He loves you and desires to have a personal relationship with you.

May I remind you—there was a time when you did not exist. There will never be a time again when you cease to exist. James asked the question we all must answer: "What is your life?" (4:14).

For a Musician

Scripture: Judges 5:3; Psalm 95:1-7; Psalm 98:1-6

Introduction: "Music is a divine art, a universal language, a vehicle of worship, and a soothing, inspiring, and saving force. Old and young, rich and poor, learned and unlearned, all acknowledge the fascinating power of music. It is as gratifying and refreshing as the breezes of the mountains. It is as stimulating as the breath of spring. It comes to the mind like an enchantment from the world of infinite harmonies where God himself is found."[1]

Our friend loved music. Music brought life and happiness into his [her] heart, and when he [she] shared the music, we found life and happiness as well.

I. **Life's music fills us with joy.**

A. **Encouragement as an attitude**

Jan Kubelik was a famous Czech violinist and composer who debuted in Vienna. He had a very successful career writing and recording music and performing in the public eye until his death. Someone wrote that he had been engaged to play at the residence of a rich New Yorker in the early 1900s, to be paid $2,000 for a few minutes of playing. But when he learned that it was for a feast, he said, "I will not play where the people are fidgeting with food."

The author of *Advance* magazine commented, "The young Bohemian evidently valued an appreciative audience more than the big dollar." His attitude toward the refinement of music was more than wealth or fame. True artists value joy of the art more than the money or fame.

    B.   Encouragement as a response

    C.   Encouragement as a determination

II.   Life's music fills us with love.

    A.   Love as spouse

    B.   Love as family

    C.   Love as friendship

Lew Wallace stated, "The happiness of love is in action; its test is what one is willing to do for others."[2]

III.   Life's music fills us with hope.

    A.   Hope is mentoring others.

    B.   Hope is looking forward.

    C.   Hope is seeking Jesus.

John Greenleaf Whittier wrote,

> *Behind the cloud the starlight lurks,*
> *Through showers the sunbeams fall.*
> *For God, who loveth all His works,*
> *Has left His hope with all.*[3]

Christian

Scripture: Psalm 1; 1 Corinthians 15:12-58

Introduction: John Welsh, a Presbyterian minister, wrote, "Those who are in Christ shall never taste of the second death; but, as to the first death, how art thou freed? I answer, thou art freed from the curse and from the sting of death; so thou mayest step on the back of death and go into endless glory. Therefore this first death is no death to thee who are in Christ, but rather an entry, or passage, or port to eternal life."[4]

Today we come with confidence that our dear friend, who had a great relationship with Christ, is now with his [her] beloved Savior and Friend for eternity!

Our friend taught us a lot about our relationship with Jesus that I think needs to be shared.

I. **This saint of God knew how to fellowship with God.**

Prayer was a natural to _____. This fellowship with God helped him [her] take hold of God's willingness and conquered his [her] reluctance in life.

II. **This saint of God lived in close communion with God.**

Prayer led him [her] to understand God's will, and living it daily was his [her] goal.

III. **This saint of God lived in fellowship with others.**

Christ made a difference in life, and there was the constant desire to help others find Jesus. That brought about coffee breaks, dinners, prayer times, counseling, and so many other opportunities for fellowship.

IV. **This saint of God relied on God's promises.**

_____'s life was never easy, but God's promises in His Word gave a firm belief in God's love.

V. This saint of God expressed the love of God in everyday life.

Everyone who knew him [her] knew that he [she] was completely sold out to God! There was never a question about that relationship with God.

I want to be that kind of saint! I want people to know when my life is over that Christ transformed me and made me His child and that my passage from this life is to eternity with Jesus!

A Great Question

Scripture: Job 14:14

Introduction: Job raised a great question when he asked, "If a man dies, will he live again?" Unless one is in complete denial, we understand that one day we will die. Death is inevitable unless Christ returns before we draw our last breath.

When Job asked this, humanity's immortality was still somewhat in question. It was not until Christ conquered death that Job's question received an emphatic *Yes!* Jesus not only defeated death but also proclaimed, "I am the resurrection, and the life: he that believeth in me, though he were dead, yet shall he live" (John 11:25, KJV).

I. We were created to live.

We were not created to die. We were created to live. Humanity's greatest desire is to live. Tragically, sin entered into the world, and death came with it. We instinctively resist death and desire life. We simply cannot accept that death is the end. We have insatiable hunger for life. God placed this desire within us.

Job sensed that even nature indicated the possibility of life after death. In Job 14:7 he said, "At least there is hope for a tree: If it is cut down, it will sprout again, and its new shoots will not fail." Just as surely as the leaves fall in the winter and the flowers fade and then burst forth in beauty in the spring, there must be hope that a person will live again.

II. Our human instincts incline us toward life.

All our human instincts suggest that we will live again. God created us in His own image. Why would He put within us such a burning desire to live if there was not life beyond the grave?

In nature we see many natural instincts within animals and birds. God placed these instincts within them for their preservation.

In the same manner, God placed within us a desire to live forever. A loving God would not mock us with a delusional desire for life and not have a plan for us beyond the grave. This burning desire to live forever indicates that there must be life beyond the grave.

III. Christ's resurrection establishes our resurrection.

Yes, we will live again. There is life beyond the grave. Death is simply a transition from this life to the next. The apostle Paul tells us in 1 Corinthians 15:20 that the resurrection of Christ is just "the firstfruits of those who have fallen asleep." When Christ defeated death and the grave, it conclusively established the resurrection of the saints.

God created us for himself. He yearns to have an intimate relationship with us. He loves us. He has numbered even the hairs of our head. We are His handiwork, the highest order of His creation.

One man, the Son of God, has risen from the dead. His resurrection reveals that death does not end it all. By accepting His saving grace, we have the assurance that we will live forever. This is not ours naturally; it is the gift of God. It is received through faith in Jesus Christ.

Paul declared in 1 Thessalonians 4:13-14, "Brothers and sisters, we do not want you to be uninformed about those who sleep in death, so that you do not grieve like the rest of mankind, who have no hope."

Our hope rests securely on the historical facts of the life, death, and resurrection of Christ Jesus. Because He lives, we also shall live. The empty tomb was not opened to let Jesus out—it was opened to let us see that it is empty.

Nonbeliever

Scripture: Jeremiah 9:21

Introduction: James Christensen wrote, "A life well-lived, stretching across the years, has come to its close. Under the wide spacious sky, in this garden made beautiful by trees and flowers, and amid these monuments of other dead, we lay to rest the remains of our dear companion and friend. May the memory of his life ever be an inspiration until the day comes when we must take our place among these silent chambers of the dead."[5]

  I. Death is an invading enemy of life.

    A. Death strikes at what we love.

    B. Death strikes at what we admire.

    C. Death strikes at what we are.

  II. Death is an unremitting enemy of life.

    A. Death never pauses.

    B. Death is always at work.

    C. Death is as restless as the sea.

 III. Death is subtle.

    A. Death lies in wait for the wrong time.

    B. Death touches everything.

    C. Death lays its hand on the heart, and the heart stops.

IV. **Death is resistless.**
   A. **Death is not stopped.**
   B. **Death cares nothing about whom it touches.**
   C. **Death is faceless.**

Conclusion: Death is an inexorable, irresistible messenger that cannot be diverted from executing its orders by the force of the mighty, the bribes of the rich, or the entreaties of the poor (Thomas Boston).[6]

Graveside Service

Scripture: Revelation 7:16-17

Introduction: We come to this graveside today with mixed emotions. A part of us wants to cry. A part of us wants to be angry. A part of us wants to feel relieved that the pain and hurt are gone.

Here are some thoughts that may help us in our time of grief.

I. **Life is fleeting.**
   Life is like dew when the sun hits the grass or the roses after they have been picked. Life is fleeting.
   How many knew the deceased for all of his [her] life?
   At what point did your life and _____'s intersect?
   Think of all that has transpired in his [her] life over the years.

II. **Life has its challenges.**
   Challenges are common in all our lives:
   Health issues.
   Marital problems.
   Financial reverses.
   The little everyday challenges of life.

III. **What are the rewards of life?**
   Look around you. *You* are the reward.

Love dominated his [her] life—and you were a recipient.

Christ cared for him [her] in spite of all the difficulties.

You and God were wonderful returns on his [her] investment in life.

Prayer of Committal

Benediction: To the God who will never leave us nor forsake us, even in the valley of the shadow of death, we give praise and honor.

Outlines for Age-related Services

For a Baby or Young Child

Scripture: Mark 19:13-16; Psalm 23; Romans 8:15-17; 2 Samuel 12:18-24

Introduction: King David and his wife, Bathsheba, lost their son. The story is recorded in 2 Samuel 12:18-24. Through this tragic story we can glean some principles that will help us deal with the loss of your child.

I. **Accept the fact that _____ is dead.**

I know it's hard, and we don't want to do it. But it is a fact in the head, even though we have trouble accepting it in the heart.

II. **Accept the fact that you will never forget this child.**

You loved your child with all your heart. Healing takes time, and you cannot absorb this loss in a few days, weeks, months, or years. You will always have him or her with you.

III. **Accept the fact that you can talk freely about this child at any time and any place.**

Someone wrote, "Talking gives sorrow wings; it flies away so you can see the sky and the stars and remember the goodness of the Lord."[7]

IV. Move forward.

Do not withdraw from life, for life goes on. David's servants were troubled by his actions, because he would not eat and spent his nights on the ground. When he learned that the child was dead, "David got up from the ground [where he had been weeping and grieving]. After he had washed, put on lotions and changed his clothes, he went into the house of the LORD and worshiped. Then he went to his own house, and at his request, they served him food, and he ate" (see 2 Samuel 12:20). He realized that others needed him and that life continues.

V. Accept the fact that _____ is in the hands of the Lord.

God did not cause this death, but God accepts this child into His loving care for eternity.

A little girl whose baby brother had died asked her mother where the baby had gone. Mom answered, "To be with Jesus." A week later that mother was talking with a friend while her daughter played next to her. She confided to her friend that she was so grieved to have lost her baby that it was difficult for her to continue. Her daughter heard the statement and, remembering what her mother had told her, asked, "Mommy, is a thing lost when you know where it is?" "No" the mother replied. "Well, then, how can Brother be lost when he has gone to be with Jesus?" Her mother never forgot the truth.

Conclusion: This child is with Jesus. He [she] is not a rose that has been plucked from this earth. Death is real. Death is brutal. Death is hurtful. Go ahead and cry and grieve; that is what we are to do. But in the lucid moments, remember that this child is with Jesus. Someday you will be able to be with him [her] again, as your life is in Christ.

The Death of a Child

Scripture: 2 Samuel 12:15-23

Introduction: One of the most difficult deaths to understand and bear is the death of a child. When an elderly person passes on, it is expected, and we often find comfort in the fact that he or she lived a full life. When a child dies, however, it seems cruel and unfair. The child never had the opportunity to experience life as we know it.

One of the first things we struggle with is trying to understand why this has happened. *Why did God take my baby?*

Let me assure you that many things happen in this world that God did not will or plan. We live in a fallen world where there is disease, decay, and death all around us. Pain and grief come to the rich and the poor, to the educated and uneducated, and to the righteous and the unrighteous. You will not find a good reason for why this has happened.

It is far better to try to determine *What.* What can I learn from this experience that will enable me to provide comfort and counsel to others who are grieving?

King David gives us a wonderful example of how to handle the loss of a young child. It is obvious he loved his infant son. We can see that he was experiencing an extremely high level of pain and suffering.

When David realized how sick his son was, he began to fast and weep before the Lord. In fact, he lay on the ground all night for a full week, begging God to spare the life of his son. The people around him urged him to get up and eat, but he refused. His grief was deep and genuine.

When the child died after seven days, his friends were genuinely concerned as to how David would react to the news. His grief was so intense that they were afraid he might harm himself. When David saw them whispering, he perceived that his infant son had died.

I. David is a great example of handling grief.

At this point in the story, I am amazed at the tremendous strength and grace with which David responded to the death of his son. He got up off the ground where he had been fasting and weeping, bathed, anointed himself, put on clean clothes, and went into the Temple to worship God. He then returned to his home and ate a meal for the first time in a week.

His friends were astonished at his reaction. It was not what they had anticipated. When they questioned David, he gave a remarkable answer. He said, "While the child was alive I fasted and wept. I asked God to allow the child to live, but now he is dead. Why should I fast? Can I bring him back again? I shall go to him, but he shall not return to me."

David found the courage to accept that over which he had no control. He realized that life must go on. Instead of hardening his heart against God, he continued to worship Him.

David knew that his son was in heaven. He determined that he would live in such a way that he would be reunited with his son when his own life was over.

David comforted Bathsheba, and God blessed them with another son named Solomon. Solomon lived a full life and is regarded as the wisest person in the history of humanity.

II. God will help you handle your grief also.

There is much about life we do not understand. Like David, you prayed, and your child did not live. Like David, your life must continue to go forward. Your pain today is overwhelming and intense. If you will continue to trust God, He will give you special grace and comfort. If you will continue to worship God, one day you will be reunited with your child in heaven.

III. God has received your child into a better place.

Your child will never again experience pain or sorrow. Your child will never shed hot tears of disappointment. Your child is happy, healthy, and at home in the presence of the Creator.

When you released your child's hand, the omnipotent hand of God gently grasped it. He will not let it go. Your child is safe, secure, and saved forevermore.

You will find comfort when you turn your thoughts toward the wonderful place where your child has gone.

We are all different, and we handle grief differently. But the God we serve never changes. He always remains the God of all comfort. If you will keep your trust in Him and His Word, you will discover that His grace is sufficient.

Outlines for Services About Heaven

A Place Called Heaven

Scripture: Revelation 21:4

Introduction: It is impossible for us to conceive an exact idea of what heaven will be like. Many gifted orators have attempted to describe its splendor. The reality is that it will be more spectacular than anything we can imagine. It is more than a silly, sentimental belief for weak-minded people. It is a real place. If we are true followers of Christ, we will one day experience it for ourselves.

In this life there are times when we grow weary from the trials, tribulations, and afflictions of living in a fallen world. At other times, our hearts grieve with the pain of bereavement. It is in times like these that we receive comfort from the assurance that heaven is a real place.

Even though we cannot fathom the beauty and joys of heaven, the Scriptures give us some exciting and enticing information.

I. What will not be in heaven.

John tells us in Revelation 21:4 that some things will not exist in heaven. "God will wipe away every tear from their eyes; there will be no more death, mourning, or crying or pain, for the old order of things has passed away."

A. There will be no mourning.

It is hard to imagine a place where there will be no tears, no death, no sorrow, no crying, and no pain. In this world our lives are often filled with heartache, disappointment, and tears.

Heaven! What an amazing place! No ICUs, no hospitals, and no cemeteries. Heaven! A place where debilitating disease and death do not exist.

B. There will be no separation.

In Revelation 21:1 we read that "there will be no more sea." The sea separates and divides. Death, distance, and disagreements separate and often divide us. We have assurance that in heaven there will be no separation due to death, distance, or conflict. The day of sad good-byes will be gone forever when we get to heaven.

While serving as president of a missionary-sending organization, on many occasions I witnessed elderly parents saying goodbye as their children headed for the mission field. They knew this was perhaps the last time they would see each other in this life. These were always tearful and painful moments of farewell. It was comforting to know that in heaven there would be no more sad farewells.

C. There will be no curse of sin.

In Revelation 22:3 we read that in heaven "There will be no more curse." The curse of sin has plagued us from the time of Adam's fall in the garden. It demeans, destroys, and separates us from God. Heaven is a holy place where there is not even a hint of temptation to commit sin.

D. There will be no night.

In Revelation 22:5 John tells us that night will not exist in heaven: "They will not need the light of a lamp or the light of the sun, for the Lord God will give them light."

Heaven will be lit up with the glory of God's presence. It will be high noon forever. We will never get tired or grow old. We will be young forever.

II. Who will be in heaven?

Revelation 22:14 says, "Blessed are those who wash their robes, that they may have the right to the tree of life and may go through the gates into the city."

A. Those who are pure will be in heaven.

Nothing impure will enter into this city. To enter, one must come by the way of the Cross. Heaven is a place for the blood-washed saints of God.

Jesus, who said, "I am the way, the truth, and the life," will be there. We will see Him face to face, and God will change us to be like Him (1 John 3:2).

B. Loved ones who lived and died in the faith will be in heaven.

I am often asked, "Will we know our loved ones when we get to heaven?" Absolutely! On the Mount of Transfiguration, Peter, James, and John immediately recognized

Moses and Elijah, even though they had never met them (Mark 9:1-5).

In Luke 16:19-31 we learn that the rich man in eternity could remember, reason, talk, and see. In heaven all our senses will be at full capacity. Although marriage does not exist in heaven, we know that every relationship will be perfectly satisfying and fulfilling.

III. Who will not be in heaven?

"Nothing impure will enter it, nor will anyone who does what is shameful or deceitful, but only those whose names are written in the Lamb's book of life" (Revelation 21:27).

"But the cowardly, the unbelieving, the vile, the murderers, the sexually immoral, those who practice magic arts, the idolaters and all liars, they will be consigned to the fiery lake of burning sulfur. This is the second death" (Revelation 21:8).

There will not be anyone in heaven with unconfessed sin in his or her life. Heaven is a prepared place for a prepared people. Whatever you do, don't miss heaven. The alternative is to spend all eternity in outer darkness, separated forever from the presence of God.

Conclusion: There was a time when we did not exist. There will never be a time when we cease to exist. Our loved ones in heaven are more alive, happy, and healthy than they ever were in this life. If we could see the place where they are, we would never want to bring them back into this world. They will not return to us, but we can go to where they are. What a glorious day that will be when we reach that place called heaven!

Death Is Yours

Scripture: 1 Corinthians 3:21-23

Introduction: In this passage Paul, speaking to believers, makes the very dramatic declaration: "All things are yours," including death. In his Philippian letter Paul expressed this thought again when he wrote, "For to me, to live is Christ and to die is gain" (Philippians 1:21). Too often we regard death as our last great enemy. Paul viewed death from a Christian perspective and said, "It's yours." We who are followers of the Lord Jesus Christ need to understand that death is not our enemy. It belongs to us. It is not our master; it is our friend.

Paul did not list in this chapter the reasons death is the friend of those who love and serve the Lord. However, it would not be difficult for us to come up with a good list of reasons that "to die is gain."

I. Some things are worse than death.

Many worse things could happen to a Christian than death. Many times when a saint passes on to Glory, it is a release from pain and suffering. Death is our friend when pain destroys our quality of life and our ability to function in a normal fashion.

At times in this fallen world, Christians experience conflicts and misunderstandings that are heartbreaking. At other times we are limited by our various infirmities and shortcomings. The holiest of saints experience many trials and tribulations.

In all these situations, death is our friend. It liberates us from all of our trials and tribulations.

II. Death introduces us to immortality.

Death is the Christian's friend because it is our entrance into immortality. To die is gain, because we will never again experience pain or sickness of any kind. Death is "ours," because tears of sorrow and heartache will vanish forever. God himself will wipe away all our tears.

When Christians die, they are emancipated from all the circumstances of this fallen world. We will never get tired or grow old. With our new bodies we will be eternally young, healthy, and happy. Death is ours, because it is when we will receive our eternal inheritance. Death is not our master. It is our friend. It will be the most liberating experience we have ever known.

III. In death we pass from death to life.

The reality is when saints die they pass from death into life. This is why Paul could shout, "Where, O death, is your sting?" (1 Corinthians 15:55).

Your loved one is now worshiping at the feet of Jesus. He or she has received the crown of life and is secure in a new home in heaven. The good news is that the tomb of Christ is empty. Jesus conquered death, hell, and the grave. Because He lives, we also shall live. For your loved one, this is not the end but the beginning of life eternal in the presence of God.

God's Perspective of Death

Scripture: Psalm 116:15

Introduction: "Precious in the sight of the LORD is the death of his saints" (KJV). The word *precious* means "of great value, very dear, and highly esteemed." It would be rare that we would ever use these words to describe death. To us, death means separation, sadness, and sorrow. We see it as a cold, overwhelming force. It invades our lives at an untimely moment and snatches from us someone we love and who loved us.

It's not often one would think to regard death as precious. God looks at death from an eternal perspective. His view is not limited by time and distance. Therefore, He regards the death of His saints as precious. He knows that physical death is not the end of existence for a child of God. It is just the beginning of a whole new life in the presence of God in a place called heaven.

Not every death is precious to God. He is grieved when a person dies unprepared to meet Him. It is only the death of a saint that is precious in His sight.

Allow me to suggest several reasons that God regards the death of a saint as precious.

I. The death of a saint is precious to God because he or she is safely home.

It's what parents feels when their child returns from a dangerous journey. There is a great sense of relief and a joyous reunion. You will find comfort in the knowledge that your loved one is safe in the Father's house. Rather than dwelling on the thought that the person is gone, think about the joy he or she is experiencing with the Heavenly Father—safe, saved, and loved.

II. The death of a saint is precious to God because he or she is eternally safe.

Satan seeks to deceive and destroy the child of God up to the very end of life. As persons of free will, there is always the possibility that we might yield to temptation. Our Heavenly Father knows we can be deceived by Satan and turn away from Him.

The moment we draw our last breath, God dispatches an angel to carry us into His presence. In these triumphant moments, God rejoices that once again the Cross and grace have triumphed. Another child of God has made it safely home and will never again be tempted or tried.

III. **The death of a saint is precious to God because he or she leaves behind a powerful witness.**

When a saint is promoted to glory, we become keenly conscious of the godly characteristics of his or her life. God wants us to take notice of these characteristics; they should inspire us to live better than before.

We are more keenly conscious of these qualities when a child of God passes on to his or her eternal reward. We should be inspired today to be more like Jesus.

IV. **The death of a saint is precious to God because his or her suffering is over.**

Your loved one will never again suffer physical, emotional, or mental pain. The day of debilitating disease is over. He or she now enjoys perfect health and happiness in God's presence. God himself will wipe away all tears. There will not be any pain or suffering in heaven.

Without question, in spite of your sense of loss, you can rejoice in the victorious home-going of your loved one. It would be selfish to wish for him or her to return to this world of sin and suffering. The good news is that we can so live that our death will be precious in the sight of God.

Outlines for Services
Honoring Public Servants

Community Leader

Scripture: Luke 10:25-37

Introduction: James Christensen relates that in Exodus 13:19 Moses took the bones of Joseph with the Israelites as they fled Egyptian captivity. He asks the question, "Why drag the bones of a patriarch who had been dead two centuries with them?" He answers his own question when he writes, "Joseph excelled in faith, in moral practice, in wisdom. They must take his bones with them on the forty-year journey so they would not forget his righteousness, his leadership, his salvation, and his faith in the dependence upon the one true God." By taking his bones, they would know they were a keeper of destiny![8]

Our friend who led our community for many years was also a leader who pointed us to our destiny as a city. We are indebted to his [her] leadership over the years, which did not end when he [she] left office to become an "ordinary" citizen.

The indebtedness includes—

I. Taking responsibility and courage to new levels.

Taking risks is not easy, but with his [her] courage, he [she] did just that. The risk was accomplished with a sense of responsibility that had the people of our city at heart, and it took courage to fight through the lethargy that pervaded at the time.

II. Taking righteousness and fairness to new levels.

The thesaurus gives us a clear understanding of righteousness when it translates *righteousness* with words like *virtue, justice, decency, honesty, uprightness,* and *morality.* This is the type of life each of us should live and includes anyone who is a public figure and leader of any community.

Equality and fairness were uppermost in his [her] mind on all issues, even when misinterpreted and misunderstood. He [She] wanted everyone to be treated with dignity and equality no matter where they came from in society. He [She] wanted the best for this community.

III. Taking magnanimity and forgiveness to new levels.

The generosity of spirit spoke loudly and clearly to everyone whose lives he [she] touched. When wronged, he

[she] reached out with a forgiving attitude that crossed all barriers. Each of us should have that kind of spirit. Let's take his [her] example.

IV. Taking patience and self-control to new levels.

This friend of ours modeled for us patience and self-control during some debates and decisions that were highly explosive in our community. I'm sure there were times when he [she] was tempted to lash out but was able to be patient and self-controlled under the heat of words and actions. That is a great lesson in life for us.

All of these we give thanks for in the life of our dear friend and hope to learn from him [her] and take these lessons with us for our lives.

Public Safety Officer Killed in the Line of Duty

Scripture: 1 Peter 2:19-25; Psalm 56:3-4; 2 Samuel 22:2-3

Introduction: We are here to stand with this grieving family in honoring the life of one of our finest public servants.

_____ answered the final call to serve all of us.

Jesus said there is no greater love shown than in laying down one's life for others. That is what _____ did for us.

This was not just a person in a uniform; this was a beloved _____ [son, daughter, husband, wife, father, mother, friend, family member].

We also gather to express appreciation for those of you who served alongside _____. As citizens of this nation and this community, we want to show our support for what you do for us on a daily basis. We honor your authority, and we pledge to stand with you in carrying out your duties.

_____'s life serves as an awesome reminder to each of us.

I.   A reminder of the courage of a public servant.
     A. Public servants make us safe, even when their own lives are at risk.
     B. Public servants maintain order, even when they face chaos and trauma.
     C. Public servants inspire us to serve, even when they model the cost of service.

Illustration: In a recording of his last sermon at Ebenezer Baptist Church in Atlanta, which was played at his funeral, Martin Luther King Jr. said, "If any of you are around when I meet my day, I don't want a long funeral. . . . I'd like someone to mention that day that Martin Luther King Jr. tried to give his life serving others."[9]

We remember _____ as one who served others.

II. A reminder of the characteristics of a public servant.
     A. Responsibility to the community.
     B. Integrity in carrying out the duties assigned.
     C. Respect for the people he or she served.
     D. Concern for the hurting or vulnerable he or she swore to protect.

Illustration: United States Ambassador Adlai Stevenson said that patriotism "is not a short, frenzied outburst of emotion, but the tranquil and steady dedication of a lifetime."[10]

III. A reminder of the creeds of a public servant.
     A. The belief in the law of God as the source of every earthly law.
     B. A belief in the law of the land as the source of every orderly society.
     C. A belief in the rights of others as the source of every act of decency.

Illustration: After the death of champion golfer Payne Stewart in a plane crash, a fellow golfer memorialized him in his next tournament. Instead of taking his driver to the first tee, the friend and colleague took his putter. The fans wondered why he stood by the golf ball on a tee with a putter in his hand. He announced, "This is for Payne," and hit the ball fewer than a hundred yards down the fairway. In a tournament where each stroke could mean thousands in prize money, he was willing to sacrifice the stroke to honor his beloved friend. Honoring a friend was more important than a golf score.

Benediction: 2 Corinthians 13:14

Outlines for Services in Crisis Situations

Suicide

Scripture: Psalm 130:1-2, 5-7; Psalm 119:169-170

Introduction: We have approached this day as a thirsty people crying out for rain, as hungry hearts yearning and needing love, as lonely, frightened individuals in the wilderness. We are seeking to hide in the arms of God as we pass through this tragic time with the death of our friend. We come today with so many questions about why this has happened.

We need to hear the voice of our Heavenly Father as He calls to us, "Come to me, all who are weary and hurting with heavy hearts. I will give you peace. I will give you healing."

Each of us has come to express condolences to the family and to be merciful to those upon whom this tragedy has fallen. Today is an appropriate day and time to display mercy. What lessons can we learn from this tragedy? How should we have had mercy?

I. **Mercy is concern for people in misery.**

It means helping those who hurt, those who suffer the distressing blows of adversity. If we find people who are hurting and in need, we should be there for them to talk to, lean on, and share their concerns.

II. **Mercy is concern for people's emotional lives.**

What killed our friend was the instrument of death, but there are things that destroy emotional and mental stability. Often there is a cry from the heart for help.

A. **There is lack of self-confidence.**

B. **There is self-imposed loneliness.**

C. **There is depression.**

D. **There is obsession that holds like barbed wire.**

III. **Mercy is recalling the good memories of our friend's life.**

At the funeral of a man who had committed suicide, his daughter stood up at the end of the service and said, "My father was a good man with a big heart. He influenced all of us here in positive, constructive ways, and we should never forget it. True, he had periods of depression when he was terribly blue and down and lost the zest for life. Apparently, it was such a mental state that led to his death. I want you all to remember his good qualities. We ask for your understanding and God's mercy upon his loss of emotional control that ended his life. But remember, please, his good qualities."[11]

Benediction: Psalm 51:10

Cancer Victim

Scriptures: Matthew 22:31-32; John 11:25-26; Ecclesiastes 3:1-8; 1 Corinthians 13:13

Introduction: Today we come to pay our final tribute of respect and love for our _____ [spouse, parent, grandparent, child, friend, loved one]. Cancer has once again claimed a life, but not before this life affected each of us in a profound and marvelous way.

Our friend would encourage each of us to heed the warning signs of cancer and to fight it as long and as hard as possible. Those signs include fever, fatigue, lump or thickening that can be felt under the skin, pain, unintentional weight changes, skin changes such as yellowing, darkening, or redness of the skin, sores that won't heal, changes to existing moles, persistent cough, difficulty swallowing, hoarseness, persistent indigestion or discomfort after eating, or changes in bowel or bladder habits. He [she] would and did encourage each of us to see a doctor.

Cancer, as any other disease, can take health, dignity, and life. But it can never take our faith, hope, and love!

I. Celebrate faith that strengthens.
   A. Faith in a loving God: 1 Peter 5:7; Hebrews 13:5; Psalm 46
   B. Faith in the Savior, Jesus: Matthew 28:20
   C. Faith in the Bible, which leads us to God. Pledge to the Bible that children use.

II. Celebrate hope that remains.
   A. Hope that remains for eternity: John 11:25
   B. Hope that gives us heaven: John 14:1-4
   C. Hope that gives us salvation: John 3:16

III. Celebrate love that is the greatest.
   A. Love experienced by all of us.
   B. Love experienced in God: Romans 8:38-39
   C. Love experienced through the Holy Spirit.

IV. Celebrate the memory that is left.

    A. Celebrate the happy times.

    B. Celebrate the special times.

    C. Celebrate the family times.

V. Claim your heritage.

    A. The heritage of respect.

    B. The heritage of dignity.

    C. The heritage of honor.

Conclusion: Carry on the good things you have inherited. There is no better way to honor the one we have lost.

It's Not Forever (Long-term Illness)

Scripture: 1 Peter 5:10

Introduction: When we are experiencing great sorrow and loss, there is a tendency to ask why God is allowing this to happen, what we have done to deserve such grief and pain.

It is important to understand that many of the trials and tribulations we experience are not the result of how good or evil we have been. This idea comes from an old pagan belief that whenever we are suffering, God is angry with us and is punishing us. However, this usually is not the case.

We live in a fallen world under the curse of sin. Therefore, in this life we will always experience pain, weariness, disease, and death. We do not have to look for some strange, mystical reason that people get sick and die. It is life in a fallen world. Adversity comes to the righteous and the unrighteous alike.

God never promised us an easy road. However, He did promise that His grace would be sufficient. Jesus said, "In this world you will have trouble" (John 16:33).

Although it is very human to ask the question *Why?* we will never find a satisfactory answer in this life. It would be far more profitable to ask other questions: *What? How? What can I learn from this experience that will enable me to be more Christlike? How can I use what I learn from this experience to be a greater blessing to others?*

One thing we know is that Romans 8:28 is always true. "We know that all things work together for good to those who love God, to those who are the called according to His purpose" (NKJV).

I. Peter's perspective on suffering.

Peter puts suffering in its proper perspective in this passage. He tells us that when we compare our present suffering to eternal glory, it's "just for a while." It will not last forever.

It doesn't seem that way when the night is dark, the valley is deep, the pain is persistent, and the heart is breaking. But one day the sun will shine again, and the pain will diminish. It will not last forever.

If we can keep this perspective, the trials of life can become blessings rather than curses. Peter assures us that God will restore us through suffering.

II. Suffering can restore us.

The word *suffer* means "to supply that which is missing." It is also the word used for "to set a fracture." In Mark 1:19 it is used in the phrase "mending the nets."

At times it seems as if life's sorrows and trials will break us into pieces. However, if we accept adversity with humility and trust, the very opposite is true. God will mend the fractures and heal the broken heart. He will put us back together better and stronger than before.

Suffering can add to a person's character that which is missing. It can repair existing weaknesses. Christ is the master Carpenter. He wants to make great saints out of us. Whatever God allows to come into our lives has the potential of being for our good.

III. Suffering can make us strong.

There is something powerful about faith that has gone through pain and suffering and emerged burning more brightly. Suffering can make one stronger, like a rock, or it can crush one.

My prayer is that your faith will be so strong that all the blasts of hell and the storms of life will not be able to defeat you. They will only serve to make your character like an inscription chiseled into the rock.

IV. Suffering can make you firm and steadfast.

These words carry the thought of "laying the foundation." It is only when we face the trials of life that we are driven down to the bedrock of our faith. It is in these moments we discover the things that can be shaken and the things that cannot be shaken.

When life caves in around us, we discover what is simply tinsel and trappings and what is essential. When we experience the sorrow of bereavement and loss, we discover what in life matters most.

With a perspective like Peter's, we can avoid bitterness and resentment. Instead of our faith being shattered, it will be strengthened. Suffering: it's just for a while.

Outline for Service Honoring a Wife

She Dressed Well

Scripture: Proverbs 31:10-31

Introduction: We have gathered to celebrate the life of a woman who knew how to dress well. She was clothed with strength and dignity. Solomon, considered to be the wisest man ever to live, described such a woman with vivid language. He begins by stating that a virtuous and capable wife is more precious than rubies. He then writes about the various ways one can determine the value of a good wife.

I. We see her value as a wife.

Solomon said, "Her husband can trust her, and she will enrich his life." Such a woman is never manipulative or deceitful. She is fiercely loyal to her husband and would never betray him.

Martin Luther said, "The greatest gift of God is a pious, amiable spouse, who fears God, loves her home and with whom one can live in perfect trust and confidence."[12]

The one whose life we celebrate today was that kind of wife. She was trustworthy, and she blessed her husband in many ways.

II. We see her value to her family.

The value of such a woman can also be seen in the way she relates to her family. Powerful forces in our world today belittle the role of wife and mother. This has had a destructive influence on our society.

Someone has said, "If you want a picture of the next generation, look at the mothers of this generation; their values, standards, and convictions will be reflected in their children."[13]

The woman whose life we celebrate today led her family in the right direction. She made certain they were clothed, fed, protected, and loved. She was a good mother. Her children all stand today to bless her as a wonderful mother.

III. We see her value in the way she blessed others.

The value of this woman dressed with strength and dignity can also be seen in the way she blesses others. Solomon said, "She extends a helping hand to the poor and opens her arms to the needy." Quietly and without fanfare, she reaches out to meet the needs of the poor and needy. That same quality was seen in the one whose life we celebrate today. She cared not only for her family but also for the needs of hurting, broken people. Only eternity will reveal the number of lives she touched in a positive way.

IV. We see the value of her hope.

In verse 25 Solomon describes such a woman as one who had hope. Her hope in God was so deep that she could laugh and rejoice as she faced the future. She knew she belonged to God and that He was in control of her life. She knew that in spite of any difficulties she could trust in the Lord.

V. We see the value of her reward.

Her reward is described in verse 28. "Her children arise and call her blessed, her husband also praises her." There's no greater reward a wife and mother could have than that—other than eternal life. To have those she loved most and who knew her best say such wonderful things is a reward greater than fame and fortune. Your loved one dressed with dignity and strength and lived well. We all stand today and bless her name and memory.

VI. We see the secret of her life.

In verse 30 Solomon gives us the secret of her life: she fears God. The fear of the Lord is the foundation for all success and excellence in life. Your loved one was a good woman who feared God and kept His commandments. Her reward today far exceeds anything we can imagine.

You have a priceless heritage! It is worth far more than fame or wealth. Don't waste it—pass it on to others.

Outline for Service Honoring a Husband

The Steps of a Good Man

Scripture: Psalm 37:23-29

Introduction: The psalmist declared, "The steps of a good man are ordered [established] by the LORD, and He delights in his way" (NKJV). When people earnestly seek divine direction for their lives and then follow that direction, the Lord will establish their steps. It is a blessed experience to see godly believers come down to the end of life's journey and observe how the Lord has directed their steps. It is inspiring and challenging for the living.

In this memorial service we will look at the steps taken by this godly man. His steps were truly ordered by the Lord.

I. He stepped into salvation.

The most important step this good man ever took was when he repented of his sins and accepted Christ as his personal Savior. Since taking that step many years ago, he has never looked back. He continued to grow in grace and Christian maturity. He has lived a Christ-centered, holy life. His faithful witness has influenced numerous lives.

This is the most important step any of us will ever take. If you have not taken the step of salvation, I urge you to do it today.

II. He stepped into service.

Here is a man that God has used in Christian service in numerous ways. He understood that we are saved not to sit but to serve. He had a servant's heart. He served effectively on the front lines and behind the scenes. Without question, he will be richly rewarded.

Far too many expect the church to meet their needs, and they come to be blessed. This brother understood that he was under a mandate to serve. He did not attend church to be an observer or critic. He rolled up his sleeves, jumped into the fray, and went to work. He did not serve for the applause but to honor and please the Lord. He loved people, and his deepest desire was to serve them in some way.

He leaves a great gap in the work of the church. Who will step up today and fill that gap?

III. He stepped into the sanctity of marriage.

He was a faithful husband and devoted father. As a spiritual leader, he set a wonderful example for his family. He didn't just send his children to church—he brought them with him.

He will be greatly missed by his family. He was always dependable and available for them. His prayers, wise counsel, and example leave a tremendous legacy for his family.

You can choose a role model from famous celebrities, but you will never have a better role model than that of your father. His steps were established by the Lord.

IV. He stepped into glory.

Several days ago this godly man stepped out of this life into the glory of heaven. He now breathes celestial air. The hand he now touches is the hand of God.

If you could see him now, you would never want to call him back into this sin-cursed world. He is home. He is healthy. He is happy and fulfilled.

Conclusion: If you will allow the Lord to guide your steps, one day there will be great reunion in the city of God. My prayer is that your family circle will be unbroken. You can have eternity to celebrate complete victory over the world, the flesh, and the devil. May your steps be established by the Lord.

9

Poems and Other Readings

Often in the delivering of the eulogy or pastor homily, an appropriate time will be provided to share a bit of classic or contemporary poetry. The following are a few examples that may serve admirably.

A Song of Living

Because I have loved life, I shall have no sorrow to die.
I give a share of my soul to the world where my course is run.
I know that another shall finish the task I must leave undone.
I know that no flower, no flint was in vain on the path I trod.
As one looks on a face through a window, through life I have looked on God.
Because I have loved life, I shall have no sorrow to die.[1]

—Amelia Josephine Burr

What Is Dying?

I am standing on the sea shore.
A ship sails and spreads her white sails to the morning breeze and starts for the ocean.
She is an object of beauty, and I stand watching her till at last she fades on the horizon, and someone at my side says, "She is gone."
Gone where?

Gone from my sight—that is all;
She is just as large in the masts, hull and spars as she was
    when I saw her,
and just as able to bear her load of living freight to its desti-
    nation.
The diminished size and total loss of sight is in me, not in
    her,
and just at the moment when someone at my side says, "She
    is gone,"
there are others who are watching her coming,
and other voices take a glad shout: "There she comes,"
And that is dying.[2]

—Bishop Brent (1862-1926)

Crossing the Bar

Sunset and evening star,
    And one clear call for me!
And may there be no moaning of the bar,
    When I put out to sea,

But such a tide as moving seems asleep,
    Too full for sound and foam,
When that which drew from out the boundless deep
    Turns again home.

Twilight and evening bell,
    And after that the dark!
And may there be no sadness or farewell,
    When I embark;

For tho' from out our bourne of Time and Place
    The flood may bear me far,
I hope to see my Pilot face to face.
    When I have crossed the bar.[3]

—Alfred, Lord Tennyson

Prayer of Faith

We trust that beyond absence there is a presence.

That beyond the pain there can be healing.

That beyond the brokenness there can be wholeness.

That beyond the anger there may be peace.

That beyond the hurting there may be forgiveness.

That beyond the silence there may be the word.

That beyond the word there may be understanding.

That through understanding there is love.[4]

—Author unknown

Music and Grief

Nothing speaks to the soul like music. In every passage of life, it is the expression of the heart. Music is a vital part of the grieving experience. Families honor their loved one with a favorite song or artist and draw comfort from beloved hymns.

With more funerals taking place in the mortuary, digital music is being used more often than acoustical instruments. This, of course, gives a wider range of options to the family but may contribute to a less personal touch. Yet the dignity and elegance of music offered by an accomplished organist may still play an important part in the funeral if the family desires.

Music has strong importance because it facilitates healthy grief. As soft music begins to play, the family and friends are invited to release their emotions, and this is good. While humans were not originally created to experience grief, we must deal with it appropriately since it is part of our world.

Often a pastor deals with a family who is unchurched and needs some help in selecting music for the service. The songs listed below are in the public domain and are appropriate for funerals. Of course, there will always be meaningful contemporary songs that the family may desire, but it is a good thing if the minister can direct them to sacred choices if possible.

Songs

All the following songs are available online.[5]

A Mighty Fortress Is Our God

A mighty fortress is our God,
   A bulwark never failing;
Our helper He, amid the flood
   Of mortal ills prevailing:
For still our ancient foe
Doth seek to work us woe;
His craft and power are great,
And, armed with cruel hate,
On earth is not his equal.

That word above all earthly powers,
   No thanks to them, abideth;
The Spirit and the gifts are ours
   Through Him Who with us sideth:
Let goods and kindred go,
This mortal life also;
The body they may kill:
God's truth abideth still,
His kingdom is forever.

—Martin Luther

Abide with Me

Abide with me; fast falls the eventide;
The darkness deepens; Lord with me abide.
When other helpers fail and comforts flee,
Help of the helpless, O abide with me.

Swift to its close ebbs out life's little day;
Earth's joys grow dim; its glories pass away;
Change and decay in all around I see;
O Thou who changest not, abide with me.

I fear no foe, with Thee at hand to bless;
Ills have no weight, and tears no bitterness.
Where is death's sting? Where, grave, thy victory?
I triumph still, if Thou abide with me.

Hold Thou Thy cross before my closing eyes;
Shine through the gloom and point me to the skies.
Heaven's morning breaks, and earth's vain shadows flee;
In life, in death, O Lord, abide with me.

—Henry F. Lyte

Amazing Grace

Amazing grace! How sweet the sound
That saved a wretch like me!
I once was lost, but now am found;
Was blind, but now I see.

'Twas grace that taught my heart to fear
And grace my fears relieved.
How precious did that grace appear
The hour I first believed!

Through many dangers, toils and snares
I have already come.

'Tis grace hath brought me safe thus far,
And grace will lead me home.

When we've been there ten thousand years,
Bright, shining as the sun,
We've no less days to sing God's praise
Than when we'd first begun!
—John Newton

He Leadeth Me

He leadeth me, O blessed thought!
O words with heav'nly comfort fraught!
Whate'er I do, where'er I be,
Still 'tis God's hand that leadeth me.

He leadeth me; He leadeth me.
By His own hand He leadeth me.
His faithful follower I would be,
For by His hand He leadeth me.

And when my task on earth is done,
When by Thy grace the vict'ry's won,
E'en death's cold wave I will not flee,
Since God through Jordan leadeth me.
—Joseph H. Gilmore

It Is Well With My Soul

When peace like a river attendeth my way,
When sorrows like sea billows roll,
Whatever my lot, Thou has taught me to say,
"It is well, it is well with my soul."

It is well (It is well) with my soul (with my soul),
It is well, it is well with my soul.

And, Lord, haste the day when my faith shall be sight,
The clouds be rolled back as a scroll,
The trump shall resound and the Lord shall descend,
Even so—it is well with my soul.
—Horatio G. Spafford

The Solid Rock

My hope is built on nothing less
Than Jesus' blood and righteousness.
I dare not trust the sweetest frame,
But wholly lean on Jesus' name.

On Christ, the solid Rock, I stand;
All other ground is sinking sand.
All other ground is sinking sand.

His oath, His covenant, His blood,
Support me in the whelming flood.
When all around my soul gives way,
He then is all my hope and stay.

When He shall come with trumpet sound,
May I then in Him be found!
Dressed in His righteousness alone,
Faultless to stand before the throne!
—Edward Mote

Nearer, My God, to Thee

Nearer, my God, to Thee,
Nearer to Thee!
E'en though it be a cross
That raiseth me,
Still all my song shall be:
Nearer, my God, to Thee;

Nearer, my God, to Thee,
Nearer to Thee!

There let the way appear,
Steps unto heav'n;
All that Thou sendest me,
In mercy given;
Angels to beckon me
nearer, my God, to Thee;
Nearer, my God, to Thee,
Nearer to Thee!

Then, with my waking thoughts
Bright with Thy praise,
Out of my stony griefs
Bethel I'll raise;
So by my woes to be
Nearer, my God, to Thee.
Nearer, my God, to Thee,
Nearer to Thee!
—Sarah F. Adams

Near the Cross

Jesus, keep me near the cross.
There a precious fountain,
Free to all, a healing stream
Flows from Calvary's mountain.

In the cross, in the cross
Be my glory ever,
Till my raptured soul shall find
Rest beyond the river.

Near the cross I'll watch and wait,
Hoping, trusting ever,

Till I reach the golden strand,
Just beyond the river.
—Fanny J. Crosby

Rock of Ages

Rock of Ages, cleft for me,
Let me hide myself in Thee.
Let the water and the blood,
From Thy wounded side which flowed,
Be of sin the double cure,
Save from wrath and make me pure.

While I draw this fleeting breath,
When mine eyes shall close in death,
When I soar to worlds unknown,
And behold Thee on Thy throne,
Rock of Ages, cleft for me,
Let me hide myself in Thee.
—Augustus M. Toplady

What a Friend We Have in Jesus

What a Friend we have in Jesus
All our sins and griefs to bear!
What a privilege to carry
Everything to God in prayer!
O what peace we often forfeit,
O what needless pain we bear,
All because we do not carry
Everything to God in prayer!

Have we trials and temptations?
Is there trouble anywhere?
We should never be discouraged;
Take it to the Lord in prayer.
Can we find a friend so faithful

Who will all our sorrows share?
Jesus knows our every weakness;
Take it to the Lord in prayer!

Are we weak and heavy laden,
Cumbered with a load of care?
Precious Savior, still our refuge,
Take it to the Lord in prayer.
Do thy friends despise, forsake you?
Take it to the Lord in prayer.
In His arms He'll take and shield thee;
Thou wilt find a solace there.

Blessed Savior, Thou hast promised,
Thou wilt all our burdens bear.
May we ever, Lord, be bringing
All to Thee in earnest prayer.
Soon in glory bright, unclouded,
There will be no need for prayer.
Rapture, praise and endless worship
Will be our sweet portion there.
　　　　　　　　　　　—Joseph M. Scriven

Illustrations

No Need for Lamps When the Morning Comes

A man turned to the Lord after a rough life in his early years. One day he met an old drinking buddy who criticized him for becoming a Christian.

In his defense, the man, who was a lamplighter, told his friend, "When I go round turning out the lights, I look back, and the road over which I've been walking is all darkness, and that's what my past is like.

"I look on in front and there's a long row of twinkling lights to guide me, and that's what the future is since I found Jesus."

"Yes," his friend replied, "but eventually you get to the last lamp and turn it out, and where are you then?"

"Then? Why, when the last lamp goes out, it's dawn, and there ain't no need for lamps when the morning comes."[1]

Made for the Skies

Sören Kierkegaard, the Danish philosopher, told a story about a goose who was wounded and landed in a barnyard with some chickens. He played with the chickens, ate with the chickens, and after a while began thinking he was a chicken. One day a flock of geese flew over, migrating to their home. The goose in the barnyard heard them honking and looked up into the sky.

Something stirred within the breast of this goose. Something called him to the skies. He began to flap his unused wings and rose a few feet into the air. But he stopped, settled back down into the mud of the barnyard, and gave up. He heard their cry, but he settled for less.

Don't settle for less. God has made you for heaven. Listen for His call, and be ready to take flight.[2]

No Limitations in Heaven

Joni Eareckson Tada tells about a visit from her cousin Eddie, who came with his old 1950s-style Super 8 movie projector and a few reels of 8mm home movies. When he began showing the movies, Joni, a quadriplegic, witnessed something on the screen that she had not experienced in thirty years: she saw herself at age fifteen or sixteen.

She saw herself wearing a sweatshirt and jeans and holding onto the reins of her horse Tumbleweed while Cousin Eddie sat atop the saddle. As she led the horse, she watched herself walking on the screen. She noticed her moccasins were old and unraveling at the seams. It gave her goose bumps to think she had not worn out a pair of shoes in three decades.

Afterward her husband asked what was going through her head as she watched herself walk. She said there was a time when she would have sighed and wished she could go back to that. But now she thinks, "Wow—this is the way it soon will be. Heaven is coming, and I can look forward to having a body that works. And I'll do so much more than walk!"[3]

Not Death but Birth

Rabbi David Wolpe recalls an ancient Jewish parable about twin fetuses lying together in the womb. One believes there is a world beyond the womb where people walk upright, where there are mountains and oceans, a sky filled with stars. The other can barely contain his contempt for such foolish ideas.

Suddenly the "believer" leaves the womb and travels through the birth canal, leaving behind the only way of life he has ever known. The remaining fetus is sad, convinced that his companion has suffered a great catastrophe. Outside the womb, however, the parents are rejoicing. For what the remaining brother, left behind, has just witnessed is not death but birth.

This is a classic view of the afterlife—a birth into a world that we on earth can only try to imagine.[4]

Hope in Jesus Christ Alone

Several years ago Malcolm Muggeridge, the noted British journalist, was a guest at a breakfast in Washington, D.C. After giving his testimony, he made several observations about world affairs, all of which were pessimistic. One of the Christians present asked, "Dr. Muggeridge, you have been very pessimistic. Don't you have any reason for optimism?"

Muggeridge replied, "My friend, I could not be more optimistic than I am, because my hope is in Jesus Christ alone." Then after a pause, he added, "Just think if the apostolic Church had pinned its hope on the Roman Empire!"[5]

The Meaning of Hope

What does hope do for mankind?

Hope shines brightest when the hour is darkest.

Hope motivates when discouragement comes.

Hope energizes when the body is tired.

Hope sweetens while the bitterness bites.
Hope sings when all melodies are gone.
Hope believes when the evidence is eliminated.
Hope listens for answers when no one is talking.
Hope climbs over obstacles when no one is helping.
Hope endures hardship when no one is caring.
Hope smiles confidently when no one is laughing.
Hope reaches for answers when no one is asking.
Hope presses toward victory when no one is encouraging.
Hope dares to give when no one is sharing.
Hope brings the victory when no one is winning.[6]

No Fear of Death.

"Many people say they do not fear death but the process of dying. It's not the destination but the trip that they dread."[7]

—Billy Graham

"Jesus has taken away the fear of death for those who trust in Him. He will give us strength when we have none of our own, courage when we are cowardly, and comfort when we are hurting."[8]

—Billy Graham

"Many of the experiences in life we fear because of the anticipation, but when we actually encounter them they lose much of their terror. I suspect death is like that. Its power to terrorize fades as we near the actual moment of passing."[9]

—Billy Graham

Nothing Without Hope

"Everything that is done in the world is done by hope. No farmer would sow one grain of corn if he hoped not it would grow up and become seed; no bachelor would marry a wife if he hoped not to have children; no merchant or tradesman would set himself to work if he did not hope to reap benefit thereby."[10]

—Martin Luther

Hope Essential for Happiness.

"The grand essentials of happiness are something to do, something to love, and something to hope for."[11]

—Thomas Chalmers

Hope Is a Christian Virtue.

Richard John Neuhaus took a flight to Pittsburgh for a speaking engagement. During the drive from the airport, one of his hosts persistently decried the disintegration of American social fabric and the disappearance of Christian values. After a very tedious drive, Neuhaus offered these words of advice: "The times may be bad, but they are the only times we are given. Remember: hope is still a Christian virtue, and despair is a mortal sin."[12]

The Transforming Power of Hope

In the British Museum hangs an unusual painting called *Hope*. On the background of the canvas are the familiar outlines of the continents and oceans of Planet Earth. In the foreground a beautiful woman sits at a harp. Nearly all the harp's strings dangle helplessly from the top of the harp or lie uselessly on the lap of the woman's dress. Only one string remains taut.

A friend standing in front of the painting with Les Parrot commented on how little of the harp was still intact and said, "I wonder why they call this painting *Hope*."

Parrott observed, "The answer was clear to me. Hope is the song of a broken instrument. It is the plucking of that one string and knowing that you can still have music."[13]

God Will Take Care of You

"We forget the mercies and blessings of the past, and for that reason we get discouraged in the present and become fearful about the future. God has taken care of you up to this hour, and He is never going to forsake you."[14]

—Warren Wiersbe

God Believes in Me

God believes in me;
Therefore my situation is never hopeless.
God walks with me;
Therefore I am never alone.
God is on my side;
Therefore I can never lose.

—Anonymous

The Greatest Weapon

Winston Churchill recognized the value of hope. He was prime minister of England during some of the darkest hours of World War II. A reporter once asked him what his country's greatest weapon had been against Hitler's Nazi regime. Churchill replied, "It was what England's greatest weapon has always been—hope."[15]

No Hopeless Situations.

Battle of Verdun hero Marshal Ferdinand Foch of France said, "There are no hopeless situations: there are only men who have grown hopeless about them."[16]

The Light of Heaven

Norman Riggs was captured by the Japanese during World War II and was taken to a concentration camp in China. He watched his friends die of malnutrition, hypothermia, fatigue, and sickness. He became a skeleton of the strong soldier he once was. One day in desperation he buried the handle of his little shovel, which was used to dig in the mines, intending to impale himself on the blade.

Suddenly a ray of light broke through the gray skies. He later recalled,

> I couldn't explain what happened, but suddenly in that moment the light of heaven hit me and warmed me. I knew God was there and that He cared and loved me. A calm peace came over me, and I chose not to take my life that day or ever. Every time I felt the growing pangs of hunger that we suffered with every day, I would think about the light of heaven, and it would somehow satisfy my hunger. Every time I was weary and didn't know if I could take another step, I thought about the light and knew God was close to me, giving me the strength to carry on. Every time despair would try to envelop my soul in the darkness of night, I would think about the light of heaven, and it gave me the hope to hold on for one more day.[17]

What I Learned from Sorrow

I walked a mile with Pleasure,
*　　She chattered all the way;*
But left me none the wiser
*　　For all she had to say.*

I walked a mile with Sorrow
*　　And ne'er a word said she;*

> *But, oh, the things I learned from her*
> *When Sorrow walked with me.*[18]
> —Robert Browning Hamilton

Hello, God!

Joy Carroll Wallis, once an Anglican priest in Brixton, just outside of London, tells a wonderful story about a woman in her church. This woman underwent serious surgery, and because she was elderly, her prospects of recovery were slim. Fortunately, she survived the surgery.

As she opened her eyes, the first thing she saw was the blurred image of her doctor dressed in the typical white doctor's jacket. She smiled and said, "Hello, God! My name is Mary!"

That's the kind of assurance of eternal life we can all have through faith.[19]

What to Do About Death

There are only three things you can do about death. You can accept it and prepare for it by receiving Jesus Christ as your only Savior; you can fear it and spend all of your money and all of your time and resources running to escape it; or you can ignore it and subscribe to the words of H. L. Mencken, who said, "Death is a universal conspiracy not to be mentioned."[20]

Not Destroyed but Released

Charles Haddon Spurgeon tells of a child who once found some beautiful eggs in a nest. A week later he visited the nest again, only to run home crying, "Mother, I had some beautiful eggs in this nest and now they're destroyed! There's nothing left but a few pieces of broken shell!" His mother's reply was soothing: "The eggs weren't destroyed.

There were little birds inside those eggs, and they've flown away and are singing in the branches of the trees."

Spurgeon made the point that when we look at our departed loved ones, we may accuse death and say, "Is this all you have left us, ruthless spoiler?" But faith whispers, "No, the shell is broken, but among the birds of paradise, singing amid unwithering bowers, you shall find the spirits of your beloved ones. You see, it is not a loss to die; it is a gain, a lasting, a perpetual and unlimited gain!"[21]

Will Death Hurt?

Catherine Marshall tells the story of a young lad who was suffering a terminal illness. He asked his mother what death was like. He said, "Mom, will death hurt?"

She said, "Kenneth, you remember when you were a tiny boy how you used to play so hard all day that when night would come you would be too tired even to undress? You would just tumble into mother's bed and fall asleep.

"You knew that was not your bed—it was not where you belonged. And you would only stay there a little while. In the morning, much to your surprise, you would wake up and find yourself in your own bed in your own room.

"You were there because someone had loved you and taken care of you. Your father had come—with big strong arms—and carried you away. Kenneth, death is just like that." That little lad relaxed and never asked that question again. Several weeks later he fell asleep just as his mother said he would.

Saints, one of these days we will just wake up and find ourselves in the arms of Jesus in the room He prepared for us.[22]

Being Prepared for Death

In Mitch Albom's book *Tuesdays with Morrie* the author tells about Morrie, a beloved, somewhat crotchety professor at Brandeis University who was dying of Lou Gehrig's disease. He was very open about the debilitating effects of the disease. He was also philosophical about the fact that there are more important things in life than just earning money or moving up in one's career.

At one point Morrie says, "Everyone knows they're going to die, but nobody believes it. If we did, we would do things differently."

"So we kid ourselves about death?" the author asked.

"Yes," Morrie replied. "But there's a better approach: to know you're going to die and to be *prepared* for it at any time. That's better. That way you can actually be *more* involved in your life while you're living."[23]

In the Hands of a Merciful God

When United States President Andrew Jackson came to the end of life in 1845, he was prepared. Physically worn out but spiritually enlivened, he told one and all during the spring of that year that they should not weep for him. On May 29 he told visitors, "Sirs, I am in the hands of a merciful God. I have full confidence in his goodness and mercy. . . . The Bible is true. I have tried to conform to its spirit as near as possible. Upon that sacred volume I rest my hope for eternal salvation, through the merits and blood of our blessed Lord and Savior, Jesus Christ."[24]

Have You Hope?

"John Knox inspired the masses and defied the excesses of the throne. Some loved him, others despised him, but Scotland has never forgotten him. To this day you can visit his home in Edinburgh and stand in the room where some believe he took his final breath.

"Here is what happened. His coworker Richard Bannatyne stood near his bedside. Knox's breath became labored and slow. Bannatyne leaned over his friend's form. 'The time to end your battle has come—have you hope?' he whispered to his friend.

"The answer from the old reformer came in the form of a finger. He lifted his finger and pointed it upward and died. May your death find you pointing in the same direction."[25]

Facing Death

"Now, I know that someday I am going to come to what some people will say is the end of this life. They will probably put me in a box and roll me right down here in front of the church, and some people will gather around, and a few people will cry. But I have told them not to do that because I don't want them to cry. I want them to begin the service with the Doxology and end with the Hallelujah Chorus, because I am not going to be there, and I am not going to be dead. I will be more alive than I have ever been in my life, and I will be looking down upon you poor people who are still in the land of dying and have not yet joined me in the land of the living. And I will be alive forevermore, in greater health and vitality and joy than ever, ever, I or anyone has known before."[26]

—D. James Kennedy

Everyone Is Going to Die

A minister was visiting a country church, and he began his sermon with a stirring reminder:

"Everyone in this parish is going to die!"

The minister looked around. He noticed a man in the front pew, smiling broadly.

"Why are you so amused?" he asked.

"I'm not from this parish," the man said. "I'm just visiting my sister for the weekend."[27]

What's Inside a Person?

Dietrich Bonhoeffer, the German theologian and pastor, was executed in 1945 by the Nazis for his participation in a plot to assassinate Hitler. Just before Christmas 1944, he wrote a final letter to his fiancé, Maia Von Wedemeyer. Knowing he faced certain death, he wrote, "You must not think that I am unhappy. What is happiness and unhappiness? It depends so little on the circumstances; it depends only on that which happens inside a person."[28]

Dismissed to Assemble on the Other Side

In Abraham Lincoln's younger days, he served as captain of a company of militia during the Black Hawk Indian War. Because he was inexperienced in the formalities of military drill, he often blundered.

Once while marching a line of more than twenty men abreast, he came to a long fence with a single narrow gate. For the life of him, Lincoln could not remember the proper command to get his company endwise so that it could go through the gate.

Finally, as the troop neared the gate, Lincoln ordered, "This company is dismissed for two minutes, when it will fall in again on the other side of the gate."

Could we make this application to death? One of these days the Lord will dismiss me (my soul) from this worn out human body so that I can pass through this gate called "death," to be rejoined with others of my company on the other side.[29]

Mine Is in Heaven

In Bill Keane's "Family Circus" Dolly is talking to another little girl who has a postcard in her hand. She says, "My grandfather is in Florida."

Not to be outdone, Dolly says, "That's nothin'—mine is in heaven."[30]

Rewriting One's Obituary

Toward the end of the nineteenth century, Swedish chemist Alfred Nobel woke one morning to read his own obituary in the local newspaper: "Alfred Nobel, the inventor of dynamite, who died yesterday, devised a way for more people to be killed in a war than ever before, and he died a very rich man."

Actually, the newspaper reporter had erred. It was Nobel's older brother who had died. Alfred decided he wanted to be known for something other than developing the means to kill people efficiently and for amassing a fortune in the process.

So he initiated the Nobel Prize, the award for scientists and writers who promote peace. Nobel said, "Every man ought to have the chance to correct this epitaph in midstream and write a new one."[31]

See You in the Morning

When a sharp pain struck the heart of Peter Marshall and he was being carried out into the night on a stretcher, he looked up into the face of his wife, Catherine, and said, "See you in the morning, Darling." It is the Christian's faith that though the night be dark and long, the morning will surely come, and with it a blessed reunion.[32]

It Will Go Right Through You

A writer reporting the Walker Cup Golf Matches in Scotland several years ago said that the American players would face not only the hazards of the Old Course at St. Andrews but also cold, probable rain, and a "lazy wind." He went on to describe a "lazy wind" as one that was too lazy to go around, so it went right through you. It is not otherwise with the trouble that causes grief—it may go around you for a time, but sooner or later it will go right through you. In the world, whether you wish it or not, "ye shall have tribulation" (John 16:33, KJV).[33]

I Do Know One Thing

A sick man turned to his doctor as he was preparing to leave the examination room and said, "Doctor, I'm afraid to die. Tell me what lies on the other side."

Very quietly, the doctor said, "I don't know."

"You're a Christian man, and you don't know what's on the other side?"

The doctor was holding the handle of the door; on the other side came a sound of scratching and whining, and as he opened the door, a dog sprang into the room and leaped on him with an eager show of gladness. Turning to the patient, the doctor said, "Did you notice my dog? He's never been in this room before. He didn't know what was inside. He knew nothing except that his master was here, and when the door opened, he sprang in without fear. I know little of what is on the other side of death, but I do know one thing—I know my Master is there, and that is enough."[34]

Humorous Illustrations

Death Doesn't Have a Good Track Record

In the cartoon *SHOE*, Skyler holds up his report card and says, "I study all night and get a lousy C. And dumb Lenny lucks out an A!" His father replies, "You may as well get used to it, Skyler. Life isn't fair. But then, death doesn't have a good track record either."[35]

He Was a Saint

Two brothers were stalwarts in attendance at a local church but were hypocrites who lived a wicked life on the wealth they inherited from their grandfather.

A new pastor was called to their church. It didn't take long for him to learn about the brothers' hypocritical lifestyle. Soon one of the brothers died, and the preacher was asked to conduct the funeral.

Just before the funeral, the surviving brother pulled the pastor aside and told him he didn't want anything bad said about his brother during the service.

"In fact," the brother advised, "If you tell these folks that my brother was a saint, I'll write you a check big enough to pay off the mortgage on the church."

The preacher wrestled with the assignment, but a few minutes later made his way to the front of the funeral chapel and started the service.

"We are gathered here today in loving memory of one of the most wicked men in this community, but next to his brother here, I'm sure we can all agree our departed friend was a *saint*!"[36]

Heaven Quiz

A pastor gathered the children around him on the platform for story time. Talking about being good and going to heaven, he asked, "Where do you boys and girls want to go?"

The children shouted the answer: "To heaven!"

"And what do you have to be to go to heaven?" he asked.

A kindergarten boy's face lit up. "I know," he said with assurance.

"Okay," the pastor replied. "Tell the congregation."

The little boy turned around to the congregation and gave a one-word response: "Dead."[37]

They're Looking for Me

A little boy answered the phone.

"Hello."

A voice on the other end asked for his mother.

The boy replied, "She can't come to the phone. She's outside talking to the policeman."

The caller said, "Okay—then let me speak to your dad."

The boy replied, "Sorry. He's outside talking to the policeman too."

Curious, the caller asked, "Why is everybody outside talking to the policeman?"

The boy responded in a hushed voice, "They're all looking for me."[38]

That's Living

A man was extremely proud of the things he owned. But his most prized possession was his car, a brand-new Lexus. Loaded with every option available, the automobile was the envy of his friends (and a couple of relatives). The car had become the central thing in his life. In fact, he put a clause in his will that in the event of his death, he would be buried in that car—probably making it quite difficult to line up any pallbearers.

The dreaded day arrived, and his last wishes were carried out.

At the cemetery, one of his envious friends watched as his buddy was lowered into the grave, car and all, and was overcome with emotion. "Man!" he exclaimed. "That's really living!"[39]

Afraid of the Dark

A little girl was afraid to go to bed in the dark by herself. After three or four trips to her parents' bedroom, her father sought to reassure her, "Look, Honey," he said. "You're not really alone in your bedroom. God is watching over you. God is everywhere, and He's in your bedroom."

The little girl was not reassured. She started back to her room but stopped at the door and said in a loud whisper, "God, if you're in there, please don't say anything. It would scare me to death."[40]

Funeral Service Checklist

Pre-funeral

- Schedule/visitation/date and time/representation
- Funeral home/contact person/call
- Facilities (seating)
- Sound system/engineer
- Musicians
- Music playback
- Musical instruments
- Lectern arrangement
- Location of restrooms
- Waiting area

- Family meeting area/schedule
- Family visit
- Church notifications
- Publication announcement
- Flowers
- Memorials
- Information counsel to the family
- Special honors
- Special guests/rituals (service, graveside)
- Special requests—readings, scripture, graveside
- Sermon preparation
- Family dinner arrangements
  Location
  Time
  Contact person
  Contact
  Set-up/tear-down
  Opening/shutting facility
  Approximate attendees
  Menu suggestions
  Wait staff
  Serving plan
  Budget/buying/payment
  Notification/enlistment
- Photo/video agreement—technician, setup, supplies, delivery
- Special displays/presentations/audiovisual—setup, equipment, technician, notification
- Pallbearer list/assignment (funeral director)
- Care-giving contact—plan
- Outreach/assimilation contact—plan
- Memorials request/recognition
- Cemetery

- Transportation

Funeral

- Sermon
- Scripture request
- Song request
- Reading request
- Music selection
- Equipment check
- Lighting
- Placement
- Participants
- Order of service
- Seating
- Eulogy
- Special requests
- Processional—pre-service and post-service
- Benediction/committals
- Announcements—family requests
- Family greeting
- Funeral home protocol (procession, last viewing, farewell)
- Certificate signings
- Records /preservations/distribution
- Transportation

11

Committals

Committal 1

And now we have come to commit this body to its final resting place and the spirit into the hands of the God who gave it. We pray, O Father, that you will deal in mercy and grace with every one of us when it is our time to cross from earth into glory. And we thank you for the hope of eternal life we have through the resurrection of Jesus Christ, our Lord.

Scripture Reading: Revelation 21:1-7

Then I saw a new heaven and a new earth, for the first heaven and the first earth had passed away, and there was no longer any sea. I saw the Holy City, the new Jerusalem, coming down out of heaven from God, prepared as a bride beautifully dressed for her husband. And I heard a loud voice from the throne saying, "Now the dwelling of God is with men, and he will live with them. They will be his people, and God himself will be with them and be their God. He will wipe every tear from their eyes. There will be no more death or mourning or crying or pain, for the old order of things has passed away."

He who was seated on the throne said, "I am making everything new!" Then he said, "Write this down, for these words are trustworthy and true."

He said to me: "It is done. I am the Alpha and the Omega, the Beginning and the End. To him who is thirsty I will give to drink without cost from the spring of the water of life. He who overcomes will inherit all this, and I will be his God and he will be my son."

Scripture Reading: Revelation 22:1-5

Then the angel showed me the river of the water of life, as clear as crystal, flowing from the throne of God and of the Lamb down the middle of the great street of the city. On each side of the river stood the tree of life, bearing twelve crops of fruit, yielding its fruit every month. And the leaves of the tree are for the healing of the nations. No longer will there be any curse. The throne of God and of the Lamb will be in the city, and his servants will serve him. They will see his face, and his name will be on their foreheads. There will be no more night. They will not need the light of a lamp or the light of the sun, for the Lord God will give them light. And they will reign forever and ever.

Prayer

Benediction

May the grace of the Lord Jesus Christ, and the love of God, and the fellowship of the Holy Spirit be with you all [2 Corinthians 13:14]. Amen.

Committal 2

Invocation

O Eternal God, our Father, from whom all life flows, grant us the peace of your divine presence at this time of sorrow; give us the assurance of eternal life through the triumph of Jesus our Lord; and enable us to rest our hearts in the strength you have promised through the comfort of the Holy Spirit. In the name of Christ we pray. Amen.

Scripture Reading: John 11:25-26, RSV

I am the resurrection and the life; he who believes in me, though he die, yet shall he live, and whoever lives and believes in me shall never die.

Scripture Reading: Job 19:25-27

I know that my Redeemer lives, and that in the end he will stand upon the earth. And after my skin has been destroyed, yet in my flesh I will see God; I myself will see him, with my own eyes.

Scripture Reading: 1 Timothy 6:7

We brought nothing into the world, and we can take nothing out of it.

Scripture Reading: Job 1:21

The LORD gave and the LORD has taken away; may the name of the LORD be praised.

Minister

Inasmuch as Almighty God in His wise providence has received to himself the soul of our deceased _____ [brother, sister, child], we come to commit to the ground this mortal body, expecting the resurrection of the dead on that great day and the hope of eternal life through our Lord Jesus Christ, who will come to judge the world, at which time the earth and sea shall bring forth their dead, and the earthly bodies of those who sleep in Him will be changed to become like His own glorious body, because of the power with which He created all things and by which He forever conquered sin and the grave.

Prayer

Benediction

May the grace of the Lord Jesus Christ, and the love of God, and the fellowship of the Holy Spirit be with you all [2 Corinthians 13:14]. Amen.

Committal 3

As we stand beside the final resting place of our departed _____ [brother, sister, child], we are reminded of the words of the apostle Paul when he declares, "I am convinced that neither death nor life, neither angels nor demons, neither the present nor the future, nor any powers, neither height nor depth, nor anything else in all creation, will be able to separate us from the love of God that is in Christ Jesus our Lord" (Romans 8:38-39).

Scripture Reading: 2 Corinthians 5:1-6

Now we know that if the earthly tent we live in is destroyed, we have a building from God, an eternal house in heaven, not built by human hands. Meanwhile we groan, longing to be clothed with our heavenly dwelling, because when we are clothed, we will not be found naked. For while we are in this tent, we groan and are burdened, because we do not wish to be unclothed but to be clothed with our heavenly dwelling, so that what is mortal may be swallowed up by life. Now it is God who has made us for this very purpose and has given us the Spirit as a deposit, guaranteeing what is to come. Therefore we are always confident and know that as long as we are at home in the body we are away from the Lord.

Minister

For as much as Almighty God has, in His wise providence, taken from this world the spirit of our departed _____ [brother, sister, child], we find rest in the certain hope of the resurrection and the promise of eternal life for all who die in faith in Jesus Christ. We now commit this mortal body to the ground; earth to earth, ashes to ashes, dust to dust; in the calm assurance that on the great resurrection day Christ will transform the bodies of those who sleep in Him into the likeness of His own glorious body. Amen.

Prayer

Benediction

May the God of peace, who through the blood of the eternal covenant brought back from the dead our Lord Jesus, that great Shepherd of the sheep, equip you with everything good for doing his will, and may he work in us what is pleasing to him, through Jesus Christ, to whom be glory forever and ever. Amen. [Hebrews 13:20-21]

Committal 4

We are here to commit into the earth the mortal body of our departed loved one and to commend unto the Heavenly Father the spirit that He gave. Though our hearts are sorrowful, we take comfort from the assurance of eternal life for those who die in the Lord and the triumph of the resurrection because of Christ's victory over the grave. Therefore, we take heed unto ourselves as we are reminded of the brevity of life that we may also be found in the grace of our Lord and forever be reunited with our _____ [brother, sister, child] in that glorious land where death cannot enter and the Son of God wipes away all tears from our eyes.

Scripture Reading: 1 Corinthians 15:48-49, 51-58

As was the earthly man, so are those who are of the earth; and as is the man from heaven, so also are those who are of heaven. And just as we have borne the likeness of the earthly man, so shall we bear the likeness of the man from heaven. . . .

Listen, I tell you a mystery: We will not all sleep, but we will all be changed—in a flash, in the twinkling of an eye, at the last trumpet. For the trumpet will sound, the dead will be raised imperishable, and we will be changed. For the perishable must clothe itself with the imperishable, and the mortal with immortality. When the perishable has been clothed with the imperishable, and the mortal with immortality, then the saying that is written will come true: "Death has been swallowed up in victory."

Where, O death, is your victory?

Where, O death, is your sting?

The sting of death is sin, and the power of sin is the law. But thanks be to God! He gives us the victory through our Lord Jesus Christ.

Therefore, my dear brothers, stand firm. Let nothing move you. Always give yourselves fully to the work of the Lord, because you know that your labor in the Lord is not in vain.

Minister

In sure and certain hope of the resurrection into eternal life, through our Lord Jesus Christ, we commend to Almighty God our brother [sister] _____, and we commit his [her] body to the ground, earth to earth, ashes to ashes, dust to dust.

"Blessed are the dead who die in the Lord. . . . They will rest from their labor, for their deeds follow them" (Revelation 14:13).

Prayer

Benediction

May our Lord Jesus Christ himself and God our Father, who loved us and by His grace gave us eternal encouragement and good hope, encourage your hearts and strengthen you in every good deed and word.

The grace of our Lord Jesus Christ be with you. Amen. [2 Thessalonians 2:16; 1 Thessalonians 5:28]

Committal 5

We have gathered here at the final resting place of our _____ [brother, sister, child] to return the body to the earth from which it came and to commit to Almighty God the soul that He gave. Because we have faith in the triumph of Christ over the grave, we do not grieve as those who have no hope, but we rejoice in the sure and certain knowledge that death cannot keep those who sleep in Jesus. Therefore, with steadfast hope in the coming resurrection, we have peace in our sorrow through the grace of our Lord Jesus Christ, who is the firstfruits of those who will be raised on that glorious day.

Scripture Reading: Psalm 121

I lift up my eyes to the hills—where does my help come from?

My help comes from the LORD, the maker of heaven and earth.

He will not let your foot slip—he who watches over you will not slumber;

indeed, he who watches over Israel will neither slumber nor sleep.

The LORD watches over you—the LORD is your shade at your right hand;

the sun will not harm you by day, nor the moon by night.

The LORD will keep you from all harm—he will watch over your life;

the LORD will watch over your coming and going both now and evermore.

Minister

God is the giver of all life, and our times are in His hand. Since in His loving providence, He has received the soul of our dear _____ [brother, sister, child] into the realm of eternity, we now commit this earthly body back to the ground. For as it was said unto the first man, "Dust you are and to dust you will return" (Genesis 3:19). And believing in the mercy and grace of the Heavenly Father, we commit back to Him the spirit which was not made for the bonds of earth but for the limitless worlds of eternity. We trust in Him for the strength to continue our journey here until the day when we shall join our loved one in the blessed land of living. Amen.

Prayer

Benediction

Now to the King eternal, immortal, invisible, the only God, be honor and glory forever and ever.

Now may the Lord of peace himself give you peace at all times and in every way. The Lord be with all of you. Amen. [1 Timothy 1:17; 2 Thessalonians 3:16]

Committal 6 (For an infant or young child)

Jesus promised us, "I am the resurrection and the life. He who believes in me will live, even though he dies; and whoever lives and believes in me will never die" (John 11:25-26).

We are gathered here today with sorrowful hearts to say goodbye to a precious little one. The pain caused by the death of life so young and innocent is very difficult to bear. As family and friends, we have no words to express the depth of our grief, and though we know that he [she] is safe in the arms of Jesus, our hearts mourn the absence of the sweet smile and fragile fingers. Yet because we know with certainty that Christ is victor over death and that He rose again triumphant, we are sure that _____ is at this moment in the loving presence of the Heavenly Father and that he [she] will be raised unto life eternal on that great day and be reunited with us again and so we shall ever be together with the Lord.

Scripture Reading: Psalm 46:1-4

God is our refuge and strength, an ever-present help in trouble. Therefore we will not fear, though the earth give way and the mountains fall into the heart of the sea, though its waters roar and foam and the mountains quake with their surging. There is a river whose streams make glad the city of God, the holy place where the Most High dwells.

Scripture Reading: Isaiah 65:17-20, 25

"Behold, I will create new heavens and a new earth. The former things will not be remembered, nor will they come to mind. But be glad and rejoice forever in what I will create, for I will create Jerusalem to be a delight and its people a joy.

"I will rejoice over Jerusalem and take delight in my people; the sound of weeping and of crying will be heard in it no more.

"Never again will there be in it an infant who lives but a few days, or an old man who does not live out his years. . . .

"The wolf and the lamb will feed together, and the lion will eat straw like the ox, but dust will be the serpent's food. They will neither harm nor destroy on all my holy mountain," says the LORD.

Minister

Children are precious in the sight of the Heavenly Father. When Jesus walked on this earth, He welcomed the little children into His presence and proclaimed that those who would enter the Kingdom must become as one of them. The Scripture tells us that God lovingly fashions each little life and values each tiny masterpiece He brings into being. We may be sure in this time of sorrow that the great heart of God is moved with our grief and that He who sees the fall of every sparrow is not unaware of the passing of this precious little one.

So in the sure and certain hope of the resurrection to eternal life through Jesus Christ our Lord, we commit the body of this little one to the grave and the spirit back into the loving presence of the Heavenly Father. As Christ welcomed the children into His embrace when He lived among us, we pray that you, Father, will receive this child into your eternal arms, safe until the day of resurrection and secure in your loving presence.

Prayer

Heavenly Father, who created us in your image and who gives us the blessing of children, we look to you today for comfort in this time of great sorrow, and we beseech you for strength to face the days ahead.

We ask for the grace to entrust this child back into your care. We thank you for the gift of this little one and for showing us a little of your beauty in his [her] life. We bring to you our empty arms and shattered hearts and lean on the promises of your eternal Word.

Receive this little one into your loving presence, and hold him [her] safely in the brightness of your heavenly home. May your sustaining comfort enfold these parents; be with them as they walk through this valley, and keep them as they pass through the deep waters. Give them the mighty peace of God, which passes all understanding. And may all who are here today be assured of the hope of resurrection through Jesus Christ our Lord. Guide us in the days to come, that we may so live that one day we will be reunited with _____ and rejoice forever in your glorious kingdom. In Christ's name we pray. Amen.

Benediction

May the God of peace, who through the blood of the eternal covenant brought back from the dead our Lord Jesus, that great Shepherd of the sheep, equip you with everything good for doing his will, and may he work in us what is pleasing to him, through Jesus Christ, to whom be glory for ever and ever. . . .

The God of peace be with you all. Amen. [Hebrews 13:20-21; Romans 15:33]

Graveside Service Checklist

- Transportation
- Seating
- Placement
- Order of service
  Scripture
  Readings
  Committal
  Benediction
  Special readings

- Special honors/rituals
- Family greetings

Section Three
Ministering to Those Who Grieve

Resources
The Pastoral Call
Sample Correspondence
Ongoing Care
Outreach and Assimilation

12

Resources

Death and grief go hand in hand. For those in ministry, understanding the journey of grieving and the emotions that accompany it is extremely important.

How It Started

When the first couple took the forbidden fruit, death entwined itself inexorably in the structure of creation. Adam and Eve began to die right then, physically, the process of decay beginning to attack their bodily systems and grasp at their vitality. Spiritually, they died immediately. The soul was disconnected from a relationship with God, and no life remains apart from Him.

They grieved. They hid. They took their emotions and secluded themselves. And still, they didn't know the enormity of what had happened to the earth. They couldn't begin to comprehend that every green plant and furry creature was beginning to die. Living would never be the same. And on another day, when they stood beside a son murdered by his brother's hand, they began to understand the enormity of the price of disobedience.

To understand death is to be acquainted with unutterable sadness. We were not made for this, this weakness, this indignity, this surrender of our God-given life. And when we must stand, helpless, and witness a friend or family member succumb to the grim specter of death, our hearts have a need to cry out, to rail against this injustice, to mourn this heart-wrenching separation.

Even Christians who understand the hope of the resurrection and the promise of heaven must allow themselves to grieve properly.

While we recognize the strength God gives and the fact that eternity will reunite us, we mourn the curse of death that stalks each life and interrupts the joy of the present. We grieve, not as those without hope but as those who truly understand the magnitude of sin's curse—the price of disobedience visited upon all humanity. We grieve because God never intended family units to be broken or mothers to hold empty blankets or friends to be snatched from our sides. We grieve because we are human and must fully drink the cup of sadness when it is the Father's allowance for that day. We grieve because death brings pain, and we are only dust, after all.

No Sadness?

The trend today is toward less sadness. That may be more palatable for casual acquaintances and society at large, but for those intimately related to the deceased, it may not be as good.

- Loss demands recognition. Human beings need the opportunity to vent their sorrow in an appropriate manner. A bereaved person will never be emotionally healthy until he or she can embrace and express the grief that has overwhelmed him or her.
- Further, loss needs validation. A funeral service affirms the fact that life has ended, that something has been lost. A celebration of life may bypass the unsavory fact that death has occurred. And it is important for the words *death* and *dead* to be acknowledged.

Certainly, memorial services and tributes are in order. And a funeral should never be a time for abject despair—the family needs hope and comfort. But we must be careful to preserve the right to mourn—it is the heritage of humanity.

A Pattern for Ministering

While there is no "manual" for ministering to the bereaved, there are at least seven principles you may apply.

1. **Immediate family members of the deceased need your immediate attention.** Your quick response to news of a death in the family will not be forgotten.

2. **You don't need answers as much as you need to listen to questions.** Avoid trite responses to questions that only eternity will answer.

3. **Your sermons should be saved for the funeral service.** Three points and a poem are no substitute for three Scripture promises and a shoulder to cry on.

4. **Deaths may not occur in the families of your greatest supporters.** Your grace in the midst of grief may be the medicine for healing broken lines of communication.

5. **A leader's death needs a leader's response.** Your focus on ministering to the needs of a leader's loved ones should be as great as it would be for a newcomer (and vice-versa).

6. **There is room for only one in the casket.** All the attention at the funeral service should be on the life of the departed and the lives of those who remain.

7. **Your words will never substitute for God's Word.** A heart filled with the promises of God will naturally overflow in the environment of grief.

Resources

Resources are available to help you plan and participate in a funeral. Note: the list is not exhaustive. The information is to aid you in your own research. The authors are not responsible for the content, nor should the authors' endorsements be assumed.

Sample Online Resources

Sample obituary writing: <www.lippertfuneralhome.com>

Consumer protection: *Funerals: A Consumer Guide* <http://www.ftc.gov/bcp/edu/pubs/consumer/products/pro19.shtm>

A Quiet Refuge: <www.quietrefuge.org>

Grief Share: <www.griefshare.org>

Focus on the Family: <www.focusonthefamily.com>

Sample Books

(Authors' note: This is only a sampling of print resources that may provide resources for assisting with grief recovery and funeral-related issues. Check with your denomination's publisher for additional resources.)

The Grief Care Kit: Bereavement Resources for Counselors and Recovery Group Leaders, by Harold Ivan Smith. Published by Beacon Hill Press of Kansas City.

Hannah's Hope: Seeking God in the Midst of Infertility, Miscarriage, and Adoption Loss, by Jennifer Saake. Published by NavPress.

The Harder I Laugh, the Deeper I Hurt, by Stan Toler and Debra White Smith. Published by Beacon Hill Press of Kansas City.

I'll Hold You in Heaven: Healings and Hope for the Parent of a Miscarried, Aborted, or Stillborn Child, by Jack Hayford. Published by Regal Books.

Pastoral Care: An Essential Guide, by John Patton. Published by Abingdon Press.

Pastoral Care Emergencies (Creative Pastoral Care and Counseling), by David K. Switzer. Published by Augsburg Fortress Publishers.

Pastoral Care in Times of Death and Dying, by Danny Goddard. Published by Beacon Hill Press of Kansas City.

ReThink Your Life, by Stan Toler. Published by Wesleyan Publishing House.

13

The Pastoral Call

As a minister who has an important ministry role during grief recovery, you must lead the way in being okay with grief. It is the responsibility and privilege of the minister to serve the grieving family by offering the blessing of presence and permission. Being able to overcome the normal sense of awkwardness around tears will enable a pastor to comfort by merely being in the room with the family. Having the discernment to listen instead of offering platitudes will help the minister have a more authentic form of compassion.

Silence Is Good

Silence is part of mourning. Death brings silence—silence in the home where a family member has departed and silence in the hearts of those who mourn. We must learn to be comfortable with silence. It is not necessary to fill up the air with words. An atmosphere of understanding silence may be what is needed sometimes.

Thomas Carlyle said, "Silence is more eloquent than words." And it is true when comforting those who grieve. Rather than being an intrusion, silence can be a shared expression of sadness, a sympathetic bond. And your loving silence can be a great gift to a family in grief. They may just need to know that you are there, supporting them with the strength of your presence.

When to Be There

Families differ in their needs during bereavement. While many will appreciate and desire a pastor's presence at the funeral home, some may not. It should be one of the important questions a minister asks the grieving family. "I will be glad to be present during the family viewing time prior to the public visitation if you would like. What would best fit your family?"

Some will want the support of a minister in the room; others will feel it is an intrusion on a private family time. Whatever their wish, understanding it and adapting to their needs will make your ministry more personal and meaningful.

What to Say

- When appropriate, words can be meaningful. Yet too many times the things we choose to say may sound insensitive and glib. Even scripture must be used with discretion, because not every verse is for every situation. Proverbs 25:11 says that a word spoken at the right time is like a golden apple framed in silver—it is beautiful. And like Job's comforters, we must be able to discern when to break our silence.

- Be sure that whatever you say does not minimize or trivialize the loss the family is experiencing. Sometimes the familiar phrases we use—that they should be glad they are not worse off or that they should be thankful for the death because a greater tragedy might have occurred later, or some such message— do not promote comfort but anger.

- Since you are expected to know what to say and when to say it, it is a good idea to have a list of appropriate scriptures to use—verses that comfort rather than try to explain. It is also a good idea to keep some books about grief in your library and be acquainted with how therapists converse with those who are hurting. People who go to group therapy are drawn by the invitation to be real about their grief and the way their emotions are acknowledged and not judged.

- Rather than complex statements of comfort, all a grieving family really needs is a genuine expression of concern: "I'm so sorry for your loss" or "This must be so difficult" or "I'm praying for you." You should guard the tendency to wordiness. You do not want to appear uncaring, but your focused presence and attentive manner will be just right if accompanied by brief and sincere statements of caring.

- Let those in grief ask the questions. Don't volunteer complex explanations; the grief will distort whatever valid reasons you give. Later, when they have lonely hours to think about the loss, they will come to you and ask questions. For now, it is your privilege to walk beside them as they start this journey of grief and keep your heart and ears open so that later on they will feel comfortable coming to you with questions.

Death of a Child or Young Person

There is something that threatens to smother our emotions when we face the death of a child or young person. It is incongruous. Those who are young should be exempt, we reason. But all too often we are reminded that death knows no age barrier.

Sometimes death invades the womb, snatching those away who have not even drawn the first breath. Because the tiny victim is unseen, many are unaware of what has happened. The mother struggles to express and cope with the emotions rushing through her. Physically and emotionally, she is a mother; but the infant is a stranger to everyone else. In these times of poignant loss, you have the opportunity to convey the love and compassion of the Heavenly Father.

Miscarriage

This silent thief comes in the early days. A woman may be just a few weeks pregnant when she suffers a miscarriage. A pregnancy that ends naturally before twenty weeks is considered a miscarriage; after that time, it is considered a stillbirth. Sometimes there are medical reasons; at other times there is no known contributing factor. If the pregnancy is in the early stages, a woman may not experience serious physical complications, but emotionally she is devastated.

Understanding the sense of loss felt from a miscarriage may be challenging unless you have experienced a similar circumstance in your own life. Even then, it is easy to say the "right" words at the moment and forget that this is loss a woman will always remember.

A miscarried child is forever seared into a mother's soul. And with the technology available today, many times fathers and siblings have bonded with the pre-born child through the use of early sonograms. Though the unborn child is very early in its developmental growth, he or she has already become part of the family.

When a miscarriage occurs, the mother especially needs a way to affirm the life that she carried within her. In order to move toward healing, the family needs the chance to acknowledge that a life has been lost.

A memorial service can provide that opportunity. If possible, the burial of the remains gives parents a unique peace in knowing where their child is. Some hospitals provide a special space specifically for infant burial and even have special remembrance services during the year. Local cemeteries may also provide a special "Little Angels" garden. A compassionate pastor may suggest this when appropriate, realizing the long-term benefits of dealing properly with this kind of loss.

You should use wisdom when counseling a mother who has miscarried. The emotions she felt toward the pregnancy will affect her grief. If she was ambivalent or resentful of the pregnancy, she may experience a large degree of guilt, though what has happened is not her fault.

If the couple has experienced the difficulty of infertility, this loss will be especially difficult to bear, as they have looked forward to having a child for such a long time. Ultimately, no matter the emotional state of the family, you need to learn as much as you can as discreetly as possible and minister to them with the love and compassion of Christ.

Stillbirth

A stillbirth is the death of a pre-born child after twenty weeks gestation. After that, a death certificate is required by law, and a burial or cremation is also required.

Since the fetus is developed enough to be visually recognized as a child, the parents may have the opportunity to hold the body in the hospital. While this is a very difficult thing, many in the medical profession encourage parents to do this, to dress the baby if possible and spend a few private moments holding him or her, praying together and commemorating this special little life. There are even some photographers who offer the service of taking pictures of dying and deceased babies for the parents to keep. While on the surface this seems a little macabre, it is important for the mother and father to affirm the fact that this life existed and has value. Otherwise, their grieving serves no purpose, and if they circumvent the fact that a loss has occurred, they will suffer emotionally in the future.

Since the law requires proper disposal of a fetus after twenty weeks, the parents will have to choose what to do. As with miscarriages, there are hospitals and cemeteries that provide special lots for the burial of infants.

Most Christian parents would desire some type of service either at the graveside or in a private setting. Sometimes family members and friends are invited. This type of memorial is very sad but so important, and a pastor will surely have no lack of assurances for the parents that their little one is safe in the care of the Heavenly Father. The Scripture is clear about how precious little children are to God, and Jesus himself welcomed them here on earth.

Abortion

Abortion is a type of death often shrouded by secrets and guilt. Rarely will a woman talk to even her pastor about something so painful and private. Often post-abortive women choose to confide in another woman or a support group designed for just such a purpose.

The many centers that reach out to women with unplanned and difficult pregnancy situations usually offer workshops and support groups for women dealing with the aftermath of a previous abortion. Most of the time it takes years for a woman to come to the place that she is willing to admit that she is dealing with post-abortive syndrome and to have the courage to confess that to someone else.

14

Sample Correspondence

Condolence Letter

Dear _____,

On behalf of _____ [church], let me express our deepest condolence to you in the loss of _____. To experience the death of someone near to us often leads us to ask serious questions along with making arrangements and planning for the future. Please be assured of our prayers for you and for your family members.

Also be assured that we are available to help you deal with your loss and to make life adjustments on a continuing basis. Like you, we have found God's presence, strength, and grace to be very real in times of need. A Bible verse seems to express that wonderful resource so beautifully: "The LORD is my light and my salvation—whom shall I fear? The LORD is the stronghold of my life—of whom shall I be afraid?" (Psalm 27:1).

_____ [name], thank you for letting us share these difficult times with you. We are honored to call you our friend, and we pledge to do our very best to help you through the days ahead.

Sincerely,

Death Anniversary Letter

Dear _____,

On this anniversary of _____'s death, I wanted to remind you of my continued prayers and the prayers of the people of _____ [church]. The good memories that have provided you comfort throughout this year will be forever cherished. And the reminders of God's presence and help will forever be reminders of His faithfulness.

We pray that you will discover anew the words of the Bible: "The LORD is my rock, my fortress and my deliverer; my God is my rock, in whom I take refuge. He is my shield and the horn of my salvation, my stronghold" (Psalm 18:2).

May God richly bless you as you continue daily to trust Him. We remain available to you to help you in your faith journey. Our thoughts and prayers are with you during this time of remembrance.

Sincerely,

Christmas Letter

Dear _____,

As we celebrate the birth of the Christ child, I am reminded that this will be the first Christmas season without your _____ [spouse, child, sibling], _____. Please be assured of my prayers and the prayers of this congregation, that this will be a time when you rediscover God's strength, wisdom, and nearness.

The Bible speaks of the promise of Jesus' birth: "All this took place to fulfill what the Lord had said through the prophet: 'The virgin will be with child and will give birth to a son, and they will call him Immanuel'—which means, 'God with us'" (Matthew 1:22-23). The very birth of our Lord is the fulfillment of His promise to be near always.

I want you to know that _____ [spouse] and I, along with your friends and loved ones at _____ [church], are always available to assist you in dealing with your loss and making these new adjustments in your life.

Sincerely,

15

Ongoing Care

Human beings can bear only so much grief. The body and mind were not made to stay fixed in mourning. There comes a time when even ministers must pull away and focus on another aspect of life. This is necessary and appropriate.

Having appropriate boundaries results in longer ministry. But never forget that the family cannot separate themselves from the loss. It is there at every turn. They cannot go home to an easy chair and the mundane happenings of life without being reminded of what is missing. They cannot go on vacation and put it all behind them. Death invades the most private and precious of sanctuaries—the soul. And its mark is there forever.

You must never assume that the smiling face they present to you on Sunday morning means that all is well. You must not think that one year or two years or ten years will erase the pain.

While you would never want to cause additional hurt to them, remembering their loss and reminding them that you are praying for them in the months to come will help them know they are not alone. Not being afraid to call the deceased by name will assure them that their family member meant something to someone else.

Every family needs to know that their departed loved one had significance. As you feel comfortable remembering them by name, especially on birthdays and holidays, the family will relax to a greater degree in your presence and allow you to minister to them on a deeper level. In this way, you validate the worth of their loved one and acknowledge the fact that they are forever part of the human record. That means a lot to those who are grieving.

The Mourner's Bill of Rights

1. You have the right to experience your own unique grief.
2. You have the right to talk about your grief.
3. You have the right to feel a multitude of emotions.
4. You have the right to be tolerant of your physical and emotional limits.
5. You have the right to experience "griefbursts."
6. You have the right to make use of ritual.
7. You have the right to embrace your spirituality.
8. You have the right to search for meaning.
9. You have the right to treasure your memories.
10. You have the right to move toward your grief and heal.[1]

16

Outreach and Assimilation

Have you ever considered the funeral service to be an outreach? The death of a loved one or close friend may be one of the most opportune times to lead someone to faith in Christ and into the fellowship of the local church. Of course, great sensitivity to the leadership of the Holy Spirit is vital to reaching out to the bereaved. But there are several ways God can use the trauma of dying and death to touch the life of another.

Reflection

The activities surrounding a funeral service may be a time when survivors think about their own mortality. Funeral sermons, for example, may bring a sense of conviction to family and friends in the funeral chapel or auditorium—or at the gravesite. Reflecting on the claims of Christ offered through Scripture readings or homilies may create a Spirit-led hunger to know even more.

Loneliness

The compassion of officiating clergy or other funeral participants may serve as a reminder to survivors that their friendship is offered to the lonely. During subsequent times of bereavement, they may seek the counsel of those same persons. Friendship links may be established that may lead to an opportunity to share the gospel.

Openness

There is a critical time when survivors are more open to matters of faith. Soon the busyness of time will consume their interest. A polite but persistent presence in those persons' lives at the outset of their time of mourning can be used to introduce them to God's love in the person of the Lord Jesus Christ.

Strategy of Outreach

Led by the Holy Spirit, you can be God's person to express His love and forgiveness.

Following are some examples of follow-up you can initiate with immediate family members:

1. Deliver a friendship loaf of bread with reference to the "Bread of Life" verse.
2. Follow-up contacts. Ask permission to include them in electronic mailings.
3. Offer childcare services.
4. Offer yard work or a clean-up activity.
5. Frame memorial pictures and deliver them.
6. Invite family members to a grief recovery or Bible study group.
7. Invite family members and contacts to attend a special event as your guest.
8. Inscribe the names of deceased on a memorial (plaque, walkway, or so on), and invite family members to a dedication service.
9. Provide post-funeral transportation or shopping services if needed.
10. Invite family members to participate in a community service project.
11. Invite family members to a planned grief recovery seminar.

12. Deliver a memorial Bible—which may include a salvation plan or a list of comforting verses.
13. Provide a library of grief recovery media.

Conclusion
Current Trends in Funerals

As we have mentioned, funeral customs are ever-changing. Recognizing funeral service trends will help you make a contemporary impact on surviving family and friends of the deceased. Several of those trends include the following.

Cremation

Cremation is an increasingly popular disposition of the deceased's remains. In an article in *Christianity Today*, Timothy George, dean of Beeson Divinity School at Samford University, wrote, "While the weight of Christian tradition clearly favors burial, the Bible nowhere explicitly condemns cremation. Since 1963 the Roman Catholic Church has permitted cremation while "earnestly recommending" burial as the preferred mode of disposal. Billy Graham has noted (what Christians have always believed) that cremation cannot prevent a sovereign God from calling forth the dead at the end of time. George adds, "Whether final disposition is by burial or cremation, the Christian church should offer a funeral liturgy in which the reality of death is not camouflaged, and the resurrection of the body is affirmed."[1]

Web Casting

Web casting of funeral services is sometimes requested. This allows those who live long distances away to be part of the service. Making a videotape of the service is also a common practice. This then becomes a keepsake for the family or those unable to attend.

Bagpipes

Long associated with memorials to those in military or civil service, live bagpipe music is now being offered to families who wish to include it during the funeral or graveside service.

Balloon/Dove Release

As a symbolic way of visualizing the departure of the spirit, families are often choosing to release balloons or doves. Some feel this facilitates saying "goodbye" to the deceased and especially encourage its use for young children.

Green

With the current emphasis on recyclable and renewable, some family members—and cemetery owners—are asking for funeral and burial services that are "green." These may include—

- Bans on chemical embalming to leave the body in its natural state.
- Prohibiting coffins of metal or rare woods in favor of coffins constructed using more easily reproducible woods or wicker.
- Forbidding tall, cut headstones in favor of smaller markers.
- Banning herbicides and pesticides for lawn care; and banning gas-powered lawnmowers.[2]

Journey Through It

Grief is never welcome, but it is inevitable. Those in ministry should lead the way in acknowledging and affirming the right to grieve. They should set the example for how to act and what to say in the presence of those who are mourning a death. They should realize that there is no better time to be the heart and hands of Jesus than during a season of loss, and they should base their compassion on the example of the Christ who wept at Lazarus' tomb and their hope on His triumph over death.

We will never lay out the welcome mat for death, but we can refuse to sidestep it and, rather, journey through it with understanding and hope. And for everyone who ministers, it's a vital part of the divine calling.

About the Authors

Dr. Thomas H. Hermiz is a native of Endicott, New York. He has formerly taught church administration at Ohio Christian University and has served in two pastorates. He has also served as executive director and as president of Christian Holiness Partnership and president of World Gospel Mission. He has served on several boards including World Gospel Mission, Asbury College, and the Christian Holiness Partnership.

In recent years Dr. Hermiz has kept a busy speaking schedule. He is the author of *Holiness, the Joy, the Journey, the Difference.*

Dr. Hermiz currently serves as General Superintendent of the Churches of Christ in Christian Union based in Circleville, Ohio.

He and his wife, Ella Mae, are the parents of three grown children and one daughter who is deceased. They have seven grandchildren and five great-grandchildren.

Dr. Stan A. Toler served for forty years as a pastor in Ohio, Florida, Tennessee, and Oklahoma.

In addition to his years in the pastorate, Dr. Toler has written more than eighty books, including his best-sellers, *God Has Never Failed Me, But He's Sure Scared Me to Death a Few Times; The Buzzards Are Circling, But God's Not Finished with Me Yet; God's Never Late, He's Seldom Early, He's Always Right on Time; The Secret Blend; Practical Guide to Pastoral Ministry; The Inspirational Speaker's Resource; ReThink Your Life;* and his popular *Minute Motivator* series.

Dr. Toler presently serves as General Superintendent in the International Church of the Nazarene with an office at the Global Ministry Center in Lenexa, Kansas, USA.

He and his wife Linda have two sons and two grandsons.

Notes

Chapter 1

1. Amanda Bennett and Terence B. Foley, *In Memoriam: A Practical Guide to Planning a Memorial Service* (New York: Fireside, 1997), 11.

2. *The Perfect Stranger's Guide to Funerals and Grieving Practices*, ed. Stuart M. Matlins (Woodstock, Vt.: SkyLight Paths Publishing, 2000), 73

3. Thomas Long, "How Funerals Can Better Reflect Christian Faith," *The United Methodist Reporter*, March 12, 2010, Section A, 2.

Chapter 3

1. <http://www.arlingtoncemetery.mil/ceremonies/military_funerals.html>, accessed 2/27/10.

Chapter 4

1. Malcolm James and Victoria Lynn, *Last Wishes: A Funeral Planning Manual and Survivors Guide* (Valley Forge, Pa.: Mavami, 2000), selected pages.

Chapter 5

1. <http://www.inlieuofflowers.info/index.php?s=1>, accessed 3/1/10.

Chapter 7

1. <http://www.merriam-webster.com/dictionary/eulogy>, accessed 3/1/10.

Chapter 8

1. G. B. F. Hallock, *Five Thousand Best Modern Illustrations* (New York: George H. Doran Co., 1927), 522-23.

2. <http://www.giga-usa.com/quotes/authors/lewis_wallace_a001.htm>, accessed 3/26/10.

3. Ibid., 371.

4. *Inspiring Quotations*, comp. Albert M. Wells (Nashville: Thomas Nelson Publishers, 1988), 55.

5. James Christensen, *Creative Ways to Worship* (Old Tappan, N.J.: Fleming H. Revell, 1974), 223.

6. <http://www.graceonlinelibrary.org/articles/full.asp?id=13|19|546>, accessed 3/18/10. (Site now discontinued)

7. From author's file; no other attribution available.

8. James Christensen, *Difficult Funeral Services* (Old Tappan, N.J.: Fleming H. Revell, 1985), 120.

9. <http://www2.scholastic.com/browse/article.jsp?id=4803>, accessed 3/27/10.

10. Elizabeth Dole, *Hearts Touched by Fire: My 500 Favorite Inspirational Quotes* (New York: Caroll & Graf Publishers, 2004), 98.

11. Christensen, *Difficult Funeral Services,* 22.

12. From author's file/. No other attribution available.

13. Source unknown.

Chapter 9

1. Bennett and Foley, *In Memoriam: A Practical Guide to Planning a Memorial Service,* 117.

2. <http://www.whenimdeadandgone.com/cgi-bin/index.pl?PGE_ID=22>, accessed 3/27/10.

3. <http://funeralreadingsblog.com/readings-for-funerals/readings-for-funerals>, accessed 3/27/10.

4. Ibid.

5. <http://my.homewithgod.com/heavenlymidis2/index.html>, accessed 1/12/10.

Chapter 10

1. Author unknown, adapted from *Sunday School Times.*

2. Cited by Leighton Ford, "Hope for a Great Forever," *Preaching Today,* Tape No. 96, 1991.

3. Joni Eareckson Tada, "On My Feet Walking," *Moody,* March-April 1998, 75.

4. Cited by Jeffery L. Sheler, "Heaven in the Age of Reason," *U.S. News & World Report,* March 31, 1997, 66.

5. Cited by Richard Halverson, "Reflections," <http://www.christianitytoday.com/ct/1995/august1/5t9039.html>, accessed 3/22/10.

6. John C. Maxwell, *Think on These Things* (Kansas City: Beacon Hill Press of Kansas City, 1979), 128.

7. Billy Graham, *Daily Calendar,* (Nashville: Thomas Nelson Publishers, January 14, 1995).

8. Ibid., March 1, 1995.

9. Ibid., 1995.

10. Cited by Norman Vincent Peale, *Bible Power for Successful Living* (Pawling, N.Y.: Peale Center for Christian Living, 1993), 105.

11. Cited by David Vardaman, "Here's Hope," *Priorities,* vol. 5, no. 6, 1, December 2, 2010.

12. David Neff, "Why Hope is a Virtue," *Christianity Today,* April 3, 1995, 24.

13. Les Parrott, "The Transforming Power of Hope," *New Man,* November/December 1999, 16.

14. Cited by Jennifer Ferranti, "The Road to Hope," *Moody,* July/August 2000, 23.

15. John Maxwell, *Developing the Leaders Around You* (Nashville: Thomas Nelson Publishers, 1995), 72.

16. Ibid.

17. Tom Mullins, *The Confidence Factor* (Nashville: Thomas Nelson Publishers, 2006), 39-40.

18. <http://www.worldofquotes.com/topic/Pleasure/index.html>, accessed 3/23/10.

19. Tony Campolo, *Let Me Tell You a Story* (Nashville: Word Publishing, 2000), 204.

20. Howard Hendricks, "Memorial Service for Bea Campbell," *Preaching Today,* Tape No. 133, 1994.

21. John Maxwell, *Deuteronomy: Communicator's Commentary* (Waco, Tex.: Word Books, 1987), 196.

22. <http://www.preachingtoday.com/illustrations/weekly/10-03-08/2030210.html>, accessed 3/24/10.

23. Stephen Strang, "Our Great Heaven," *New Man,* January/February 2000, 8.

24. Marvin Olasky, *The American Leadership Tradition* (Wheaton, Ill.: Crossway Books, 1999), 64.

25. Max Lucado, *Come Thirsty* (Nashville: W Publishing Group, 2004), 45-46.

26. <http://pastorsteveweaver.wordpress.com/2007/09/06/dr-d-james-kennedy-1930-2007>, accessed 3/23/2010.

27. Mitch Albom, *Have a Little Faith* (New York: Hyperion, 2009), 231.

28. Dietrich Bonhoeffer, *Letters and Papers from Prison*, ed. Eberhard Bethge (New York: Macmillan, 1972), 419.

29. Author unknown, *The Pastor's Story File*, September 1992, 5.

30. Ibid., 7.

31. Ibid., 8.

32. John Redhead, "How Can I Deal with Grief?" *Leadership*, summer 1983, 106.

33. Ibid., 104.

34. Source unknown, received by e-mail, 12-03-09, Jerry Brecheisen.

35. Stan Toler, *The Inspirational Speaker's Resource* (Kansas City: Beacon Hill Press of Kansas City, 2009), 128. Used by permission.

36. Ibid., 128-29.

37. Ibid., 130.

38. Ibid., 131.

39. Ibid., 144.

40. Ibid., 146.

Chapter 15

1. Alan D. Wolfelt, "The Mourner's Bill of Rights," Center for Loss and Life Transition, 2007, <http://griefwords.com/index.cgi?action=page&page=articles%2Fmourners.html&site_id=122>, accessed 3/27/10.

Conclusion

1. Timothy George, "Good Question: Cremation Confusion," <http://www.christianitytoday.com/ct/2002/may21/27.66.html?start=1>, accessed 3/27/10.

2. Jeff Diamant, "Going Green When Going Under," *The United Methodist Reporter*, March 12, 2020, Section B, 1.